VOLUME 1

YOU CAN COOK ANY THING

A Guide for Newly Inspired Cooks!

EGGS, WAFFLES, CHEESE, & NOODLY THINGS

JORJ MORGAN

Images by Nick Elia

Copyright © 2024 by Jorj Morgan

All rights reserved. This book may not be reproduced or stored in whole or in part by any means without the written permission of the author except for brief quotations for the purpose of review.

Video Production by Firetower Media

ISBN: 978-1-960146-97-7 (hard cover)
       978-1-960146-98-4 (soft cover)

Morgan. Jorj.

Warren publishing

Published by Warren Publishing
Charlotte, NC
www.warrenpublishing.net
Printed in the United States

*For my treasures: Mallory, Ben, Sam, Brooke, and Josh.
Dreams become reality when you work hard and love what you do.
I wish for you to Dream BIG! By fulfilling your dreams,
you make dreams come true for others.
You are Nana's dreams come true!*

Acknowledgments

First and foremost, thank you to all my food-lovin', recipe-testin', potluck partyin', bubble lovin' friends who taste my food and want more. This makes me the happiest cook in the world!

My family: Well you guys are my inspiration for everything. From Joshie's finger food to Brookie's brownies, to Sammy's multi-breakfasts, to Ben's pizza and only pepperoni pizza, to Mallory's love of baking ... you guys are the food that feeds my heart and soul.

To Nick Elia: Man, oh man, are you a talent. Your graphics make me hungry ... Which, of course, is the point. Thank you.

To Joel at Firetower Media: You make me look like Giada. Well, close enough!

To Luca at Creative Enabler: What a technical adventure we've had. I look forward to all the places we will go.

To Amy Crowe: Well, it goes without sayin' ... I couldn't do this without ya!

To Amy and Mindy from Warren Publishing: Thank you for taking a chance on a "wizened" cookbook author for yet another spin on everything yummy.

And to hubby: Well thank you for being my ULTIMATE TASTE TESTER with your no-holds-barred comments and critiques and love of all things food, family, and friends. XOXOXO

Contents

EGGY THINGS 7
Perfect Scrambled Eggs 8
Green Eggs and Ham Scramble 9
Cheddar-Bacon Omelet 10
Scrambled Egg Muffins: Pizza Style 11
Breakfast Burritos 12
Breakfast Pizzas 13
My Breakfast Sandwich 14
Breakfast Skillet with Glazed Eggs 15
Southern-Style Huevos Rancheros 16
Poached Eggs in Spiced Tomato Sauce with Olives and Feta Cheese 17
Smoked Salmon Toasts with Scallion-Caper Cream Cheese, Pickled Radishes,
   and Jammy Eggs 18
Chicken Liver Toasts with Caramelized Onions and Scrambled Eggs 19

WAFFLY THINGS 20
Basic Waffle Batter 21
Granola Waffles with Yogurt and Berries 22
Red Velvet Waffles with Strawberry Syrup and Mascarpone Cream 23
Cocoa Waffles with Peanut Butter Whipped Cream and Grape Jelly Syrup 24
Lemon Sunrise Waffles with Lemon Cream and Raspberry Syrup 25
Cheddar, Bacon, and Green Onion Waffles with Jalapeño-Maple Syrup
   and Glazed Eggs 26
Buttermilk Biscuit Waffles with Sausage Gravy 27

PANCAKY THINGS 28
"My Way" Pancakes 29
Cinnamon-Apple Pancakes 30
Princess Pancakes 31
Pumpkin Pie Pancakes with Sugared Pecans 32
Buckwheat Flapjacks with Sausage and Maple Syrup 33

CHEESY THINGS 34
"My Way" Basic Grilled Cheese Sandwich 35
"My Way" Tuna Melt with Pickled Vegetables 36

Open-Faced Cheese-Topped Sloppy Joes	37
Pimento Cheese	38
Best Grilled Cheese Sammy Evah!	39
Pimento Cheese Sandwiches with Fried Bologna	40
Chili-Spiced Pimento Cheese with Crack Crackers	41
Pimento Cheese Deviled Eggs	42
Pimento Cheese Pin Wheels with Turkey, Ham, and Asparagus Spears	43
Cobb Panini	44
Avocado and Gruyere Panini with Olive Tapenade	45
Pepperoni Pizza Panini	46
Brisket Panini on Texas Toasts	47
NOODLY THINGS	**48**
White Sauce for Mac and Cheese	49
Mac and Cheese	50
Northern Italian Style	50
Cheese Sauce for American-style Mac and Cheese	51
Baked Mac and Cheese	52
"My Way" Ultimate Mac and Cheese	53
Penne Pasta in Pink Sauce	54
Ziti Skillet	55
Lamb Ragu over Penne Rigate	56
Bucatini all'Amatriciana	57
Lasagna Bolognese	58
Chicken Lasagna with Broccoli Rabe with Sautéed Mushrooms	60
Fiery Chili Lasagna	61
Lasagna Roll-ups	62
Roasted Beet Noodles with Red Onion and Orange-Maple Glaze	63
Zucchini Noodles with Pesto and Ricotta Cheese	64
Honey Roasted Spaghetti Squash with Spinach and Sun-dried Tomatoes	65
Roasted Garlic Compound Butter	66
A Rainbow of Fresh Pasta	67

Let's Do This Thing:

Video Demos!
Need a little extra help learning these new cooking techniques? No worries, I've got you! Throughout the book, I've included QR codes which link to my demonstration videos so you can see how it's done.

Things to Know
To work your way around the kitchen, there are a few things you need to know, like: What does *fine dice* mean? Or how do you *mince* garlic? Or which oil should I drizzle on my salad? And by the way, how much is a drizzle? Is it more or less than a dollop? Well, here are some answers to those questions and some suggestions to get you on your way to cooking the things you love to eat.

Knifey Things

A sharp knife is a chef's best tool. You need a sharp knife when you cut things. There are four basic knives to keep in your drawer. A chef's knife has a wide blade and is either eight or ten inches long—perfect for chopping and dicing. A paring knife is smaller and used for more detailed work like peeling things. A serrated knife is terrific for slicing bread and rolls. And a carving knife has a long, thin blade and will come to play on Turkey Day and for Sunday suppers. Store all your knives in a wooden knife block, and they will last you a long, long time.

A few knifey terms:

- **Chop** means to cut the thing into small pieces. If you are chopping a peeled onion, slice it in half and then in half again. Then chop the wedges into small pieces. Usually, you chop things to use in soups or stews. Chopped things cook down into smaller, bite-size pieces.
- **Dice** means to chop the thing into small, equal-size cubes. Take that same peeled onion (with top and bottom stems in place) and cut off the fuzzy end. Use your knife to cut slices from the top to almost the bottom of the onion. By not cutting all the way through, the onion stays together. Now turn that onion a quarter turn and cut slices down again, creating squares. Rotate the onion ninety degrees and cut down so the squares fall onto your work surface. You diced!
- **Fine dice** just means really, really small squares.
- **Julienne** means to cut the thing into long strips. This time, we're going to use a bell pepper. Cut the pepper in half and remove the inside seeds and veins. Cut the pepper in half again. Lay a quarter piece of pepper, cut side down, on your work surface. Use you knife to cut thin slices from the top to the bottom of the pepper. You can cut the tips of the strips to create equal lengths of pepper.
- **Mince** means really chopping so much, the small pieces stick together and become paste-like. Take a piece of that onion. Use your knife to chop the thing into the tiniest pieces possible. Then take the flat blade of your knife and move it back over the pieces to squish them together, making them into a paste. You can buy a hand tool that minces cloves of garlic and small bits of onion. My favorite tool for mincing is a mini food processor. This is an affordable gadget that chops and minces in minutes.

VIDEO: Chop, dice, and mince

VIDEO: Blanche veggies

Cooking Things

When you cook liquid in a pot over heat on the stovetop, you reach various degrees of bubbling.
- **Boil** If you boil a liquid over high heat, it will produce lots of bubbles. You cook pasta in boiling water.
- **Reduce** If you continue boiling a liquid, it will evaporate, thicken, and *reduce*. When we create sauces, we reduce cooking liquid and stocks to concentrate the flavors.
- **Simmer** If you turn down the heat to medium-low after it boils, the liquid will *simmer*. This means you will see a slower number of smaller bubbles. You simmer soups, stews, and sauces to marry the flavors of the ingredients together.
- **Blanche** You can *blanche* vegetables in boiling water. Blanching softens the veggie. After briefly boiling, you can transfer the veggie to a bowl of iced water so the veggie keeps its bright color.
- **Steam** You can *steam* veggies over simmering water. Place a small, metal colander or steamer basket in a larger pot of simmering water. Then place the veggie in the colander and cover it with a lid. The steam captured in the pot will cook the veggie to the crisp-tender stage after just a few minutes. My go-to steam method is to place the veggie into a microwave-safe bowl with a bit of water. Cover the bowl with plastic wrap and place into the microwave oven for three to four minutes, depending on how large the pieces are. Broccoli florets and cauliflower chunks require more time than string beans and broccoli rabe. I often use this method as prep for roasted veggies like brussels sprouts and potatoes. This produces a crisp outside and a softer inside. The perfect bite!
- **Sauté** This means to cook things in a skillet or frying pan over medium-high heat in a small amount of fat like butter or olive oil.
- **Fry** This happens when you use a pool of fat in a deep pot. You can *sauté* a chicken breast in olive oil in a skillet. You can *fry* that same chicken breast (after it is battered, of course) in a pot of peanut oil.
- **Braise** A chicken breast first sautéed and then cooked in simmering liquid is *braised*. This produces tender chicken and a flavorful sauce.
- **Caramelize** This means you cook the veggie in a sauté pan with a small amount of liquid until it reaches its most syrupy-sweet stage and is golden in color. You can caramelize sliced onions in about twenty minutes over medium-low heat. Once the onions have caramelized, you can remove them from the skillet.
- **Deglaze** If you pour liquid (like stock or wine) back into a skillet used to *caramelize*, and then reduce that liquid while stirring and scraping the brown bits from the bottom of the pan, you will be *deglazing* the pan. This is the beginning of a great pan sauce.

Some fun, yes?

Mixing Things

- **Toss** Use tongs to *toss* together salad ingredients in a light, lifting motion.
- **Fold** You *fold* whipped cream into a cake batter by gently sliding a spatula across the bottom of the bowl and then, in an upward motion, folding the batter from the bottom of the bowl over the batter on top, repeating until the cream is just blended. This incorporates as much air as possible, making the batter light before baking. You'll know you have folded perfectly when you can still see thin strings of whipped cream in the cake batter.
- **Beat** You can *beat* an egg using a fork for scrambled eggs, a whisk for frothy eggs, or an electric mixer to incorporate eggs into cookie dough.
- **Preheat** You *preheat* your oven to the temperature needed before you place the thing in the oven. This allows the thing to cook evenly.

Baking Things

- ***Conventional versus Convection Heat*** You can bake in the oven using *conventional heat* or *convection heat*. Many ovens have both settings and use either gas or electricity. The difference between them is that the source of heat in a *conventional* oven is stationery and rises from the bottom. The heat from a *convection* oven is blown by fans, so the air circulates all over the inside of the oven. Use *convection* heat to circulate around pans with low sides like cookie baking sheets. Use *conventional* oven heat for heavy pots with high sides and lids—like a Dutch oven or roasting pan.
- ***Roasting*** This uses conventional heat to cook. Roasting usually occurs at a higher temperature than *baking*, but basically both terms are interchangeable.
- ***Baste*** When roasting things in their juices, you can *baste* the thing by spooning the liquid from the bottom of the pan over the thing in fifteen minute intervals, keeping it moist.
- ***Broil*** Ovens also have a *broil* setting. This allows the heat unit on the top of the oven to brown and melt things. Use the broil setting to melt cheese on the top of your cheesy casserole until its golden and bubbling.

You Can Cook Any Thing: Volume 1   5

Other Things

- **Egg Wash** You make an *egg wash* by beating an egg together with a small amount of liquid (usually water). Use egg wash to brush a shine on the pastry, like pies and rolls, to guarantee your sprinkles adhere to cookies, or to seal the edges of pasta and wanton wrappers.
- **Dredge** Before you fry a thing, you *dredge* it in flour. To *dredge*, you want to dip the thing in dry ingredients and coat it on both sides. For example, you can take a chicken breast and dredge it in seasoned flour. Dip the floured breast in beaten egg then lift it out of the egg and shake it gently so any extra egg drips back into the bowl. Next, dredge that egg-covered chicken into seasoned breadcrumbs, again covering it on all sides. Now the chicken breast is ready for frying!
- **Marinade** A *marinade* is a combination of liquid, spices, and herbs. You can *marinate* a thing by letting it hang out on seasoned liquid before cooking to both flavor and tenderize it. You'll want to *marinate* things in the fridge.
- **Roux** A *roux* is made by cooking flour and butter together over medium heat until it is golden and bubbly. The color of the roux will decide the color of your sauce. Once your *roux* cooks, you add liquid to create a thickened sauce. Think of rich, gooey cheese sauce when picturing the best use of a roux.
- **Garnish** You can use all types of ingredients to *garnish* a dish. Decorating with a sprinkle of fresh herbs, a wedge of lemon, or a dollop of sour cream is not only appealing to the eye but enhances the flavor of the dish as well.
- **Dollop** You *dollop* sour cream or yogurt on top of spicy soups or stew to swirl in a bit of cool-down. For me, a *dollop* is more than a tablespoon and less than ¼ cup (4 tablespoons).

Eggy Things

DID YOU KNOW AN EGG IS THE PERFECT FOOD? Many recommend eating an egg a day because it's high in protein and contains minerals, vitamins, and antioxidants. I love to throw this bit of info around because I just adore eggs!

Preparing a simple egg breakfast is just the THING to get your day started. Lots and lots of us skip breakfast. In fact, it's kind of a competition to see who can wait longest after they wake to eat their first meal. And while fasting has its followers, I continue the tradition of my Irish farmer ancestors. For them, breakfast came early, before dawn, and was the fuel needed to do the chores that the sun brought with the day. I think my passion for breakfast is handed down through the generations. It's in my DNA. At least, that's my excuse to eat more eggs.

If you're not in the habit of eating breakfast, I suggest you give it a try, even if it's only a few days a week. You might find that your day goes just a little better with a belly full of eggy things. Here's some fuel to get you fired up!

Scrambled Things

There's no simpler way to prepare an egg than to scramble it. It's easy, it's satisfying, and you're eating in about three minutes. Woo-hoo! Here's how to make a perfectly Perfect Scrambled Egg.

Perfect Scrambled Eggs
serves 1 (you)
5 minutes till it's ready

- 1 tablespoon butter
- 2 large eggs
- 1 tablespoon whole milk
- ½ teaspoon kosher salt
- ¼ teaspoon coarse black pepper

1. Melt the butter in a skillet over medium-low heat.
2. Crack the eggs into a bowl. Use a whisk to break the yolks. Whisk in the milk until the eggs are pale-yellow and frothy, about 1 to 2 minutes.
3. Melt the butter in a small skillet over medium heat. Once the butter is melted and bubbling, pour in the eggs. Reduce the heat to low and continue to slowly whisk the eggs in the pan.
4. While you move the eggs around in the pan, they will slowly form small curds, little lumps of cooked egg. This is exactly what you want.
5. Season the eggs with salt and pepper.
6. Cook the eggs until your desired amount of doneness. I like my eggs still on the liquid, runny side. This takes about 2 to 3 minutes. But, if you like yours medium to more hard-cooked, keep on whisking and cooking. That's it!

Thing to Note:
You do not have to add the milk to the eggs. For eggier scrambled eggs, don't add any liquid. If you want creamier scrambled eggs, add half-and-half or cream in place of milk. If you are completely insane, you can stir a spoonful of sour cream into your eggs. It's all good!

VIDEO: Making the perfect scrambled egg

Once you can make a scrambled egg, you can make all sorts of dishes that will work for breakfast, lunch, or dinner. Simply adding veggies or meat to your scrambled eggs will make a skillet meal you can be proud of. Here's an example.

Green Eggs and Ham Scramble
serves 2
15 minutes till it's ready

- 2 tablespoons butter
- 1 clove garlic, minced, about 1 teaspoon
- 2 ounces deli ham, cut into small pieces
- 2 cups fresh baby spinach leaves, chopped
- 4 large eggs
- 2 tablespoons whole milk
- 1 teaspoon kosher salt
- ½ teaspoon coarse black pepper
- 2 tablespoons fresh curly parsley, chopped

1. Heat the butter in a skillet over medium heat. Once the butter is melted, stir in the garlic, and cook for 1 minute until you can smell garlic goodness. (Make sure you pay attention so the garlic doesn't blacken and burn.) Add the ham and cook for 1 minute more. Add the spinach leaves and stir them around. After 1 or 2 minutes, the spinach will wilt down to about a fourth of the amount you started with.
2. Whisk together the eggs and milk in a bowl until they are pale-yellow and frothy, about 2 minutes. Pour the eggs into the skillet. Use a wooden spoon to swirl the eggs around the add-ins. Season with salt and pepper. Cook until the eggs are just set. Remove the skillet from the heat and sprinkle with fresh parsley.

Make It "My Way":
Think of your eggy scramble as a canvas for flavors. You can power up the flavor with the seasonings you have on hand. For a spicy scramble, add just a couple of red pepper flakes. For a swimmingly flavorful scramble, add a bit of shrimp and season with a dash of Creole seasoning. Remember: it's your scramble. You can't mess it up!

Thing to Note:
There's lots of things to substitute here. Just remember to cook any ingredient that needs to be cooked *before* you pour in the eggs. Bacon and sausage are good subs for ham. Shallots, onion, and diced jalapeño peppers can replace garlic. All sorts of veggies will work in place of spinach. Don't forget the cheese. Just any old bit of cheese on top of this scramble will add tons of flavor.

Once you've learned how to make the Perfect Scrambled Egg, you can work your way up to making the perfect egg omelet. Omelets are kinda the high-society version of the scrambled egg. They are folded over eggs filled with your favorite ingredients. Here's how it works.

Cheddar-Bacon Omelet
serves 2
20 minutes till it's ready

- 4 large eggs
- 2 tablespoons whole milk
- 2 tablespoons butter
- 1 large shallot, peeled and finely diced, about 2 tablespoons
- 1 teaspoon kosher salt
- ½ teaspoon coarse black pepper
- 4 slices bacon, cooked and crumbled, about 1 cup
- 4 ounces cheddar cheese, grated, about 1 cup
- 1 tablespoon fresh thyme, chopped

1. Whisk together the eggs and milk in a bowl until they are pale-yellow and frothy, about 2 minutes.
2. Heat the butter in a skillet over medium-low heat. When the butter is melted, stir in the shallot and cook for one minute until you can smell onion goodness.
3. Pour the eggs into the skillet. Reduce the heat to low. Let the eggs cook for about 20 seconds. Use a spatula to gently push the cooked outer rim of eggs toward the middle of the skillet, letting the uncooked egg at the center swirl to the outside. Let the eggs cook for another twenty seconds and then repeat, gently pushing the outermost cooked eggs toward the center and letting the uncooked eggs swirl outward. Continue to do this until no more liquid will flow to the outer edge.
4. Season with salt and pepper. Sprinkle crumbled bacon on one half of the eggs. Sprinkle the cheese on top of the bacon. Sprinkle thyme on top of the cheese.
5. Use a spatula to fold the plain side of eggs over the cheesy side to form a semi-circle. Press the edges together to seal in the filling. Continue cooking for 1 to 2 minutes until the center of the omelet is set (dry and not wiggly). Gently slide the omelet from the skillet to a plate and serve.

Make It "My Way":
Here we go with substitutions again. All sorts of combos work in omelets. I've always found that my best omelets are filled with bits of leftovers from the fridge. Cooked veggies, fish, and poultry, with fresh herbs are held together with any melting cheese. Find your best combo and then find your next!

Scrambled eggs are delicious when slowly, softly cooked, and they're good when they're cooked firmly. But sometimes you can turn those eggs into something other than "eggy" by baking the eggs instead of sautéing them in butter. I like to create egg muffins by adding ingredients to the eggs and then baking them in muffin tins. This way, you can bake a batch of egg muffins in advance and have them to warm up on busy days or when you're craving a snack. Here's an example of one of my favorite egg muffin combos.

Scrambled Egg Muffins: Pizza Style
12 muffins
30 minutes till they're ready

- 1 large red bell pepper, seeded, deveined, and diced, about 1 cup
- 1 bunch (5 to 6) green onions, cut into thin slices, about 1 cup
- 4 ounces pepperoni, diced, about 1 cup
- 1 to 2 large portobello mushrooms, stemmed and diced, about 1 cup
- 6 large eggs
- ¼ cup half-and-half
- 1 teaspoon kosher salt
- 1 teaspoon coarse black pepper
- 4 ounces mozzarella cheese, shredded, about 1 cup
- ½ cup your favorite marinara sauce
- 4 ounces Parmesan cheese, grated, about 1 cup
- 4 ounces ricotta cheese, about ½ cup
- 2 tablespoons fresh Italian parsley, chopped

1. Preheat your oven to 350°.
2. Coat a 12-cup muffin tin with vegetable oil spray. Divide the veggies and place a little bit of each one into the bottom of the muffin cups.
3. Whisk the eggs and half-and-half in a bowl until pale-yellow and frothy. Season with salt and pepper. Stir in the mozzarella cheese. Pour into the muffin cups over the veggies. Spoon a teaspoon of marinara sauce on each egg cup. Sprinkle Parmesan cheese on top of everything.
4. Bake until the eggs are set, and the cheese is golden, about 20 minutes. Cool the muffins in the tin for about 5 minutes. Transfer to a platter and serve warm or at room temperature. Garnish with a spoonful of ricotta cheese and a sprinkle of Italian parsley on top of each.

Make It "My Way":
If you've ever craved pizza for breakfast, these muffins might soothe the beast! However, you can use this recipe to create any flavor of muffin you want. This is an "egg-cellent" way to use the leftovers in your fridge. Here are two awesome combos:
- **Steak and Eggs:** For steak and egg muffins, substitute with leftover cooked beef and diced cooked potatoes. A little fresh rosemary will pull the flavors together.
- **Smoked Salmon:** Skip the bagel and add some smoked salmon, capers, and diced red onion with cubes of cream cheese into your egg muffins for a Sunday morning treat.

It's your egg muffin, your way!

VIDEO: More muffin ideas

We've learned we can scramble eggs, stir things around them, fold things into them, and bake them over things. But guess what? We can also stuff eggs into things and lay eggs on top of things. Things like wraps, pizzas, and egg sammies. Here's a couple of my favorite breakfast egg combos. I bet they will become yours too.

Breakfast Burritos
serves 2
30 minutes till they're ready

- 2 (10-inch) flour tortillas
- 1 cup frozen, shredded hash brown potatoes, cooked
- 4 ounces breakfast sausage, cooked, about 1 cup
- 2 Perfect Scrambled Eggs
- 4 ounces cheddar cheese, grated, about 1 cup
- 1 small onion, peeled and diced, about ½ cup
- 1 small bell pepper, seeded, diced, about ½ cup
- hot pepper sauce

1. Preheat your oven to 350°.
2. Lay each wrap on a clean cutting board or other work surface.
3. Divide the potatoes between the wraps, spooning them down the center of the wrap from top to bottom and leaving a 1-inch border. Top the potatoes with the sausage, eggs, and cheddar cheese. Sprinkle with diced onion and peppers and drizzle hot pepper sauce over everything.
4. Fold the bottom third of the wrap over the filling then fold over both sides. Roll the burrito toward the top, sealing the filling in the middle.
5. Wrap each burrito in aluminum foil.
6. Place in the oven to warm through, about 15 minutes.
7. Cut the wrap in half and dig in!

VIDEO: Folding a burrito.

Once you can make a scrambled egg, you can make all sorts of dishes that will work for breakfast, lunch, or dinner. Simply adding veggies or meat to your scrambled eggs will make a skillet meal you can be proud of. Here's an example.

Breakfast Pizzas
serves 4
20 minutes till they're ready

- 1 tablespoon olive oil
- 4 to 6 baby potatoes, cooked, diced into ¼-inch pieces, about 1 cup
- ½ large poblano pepper, seeded and deveined, diced into ¼-inch pieces, about ½ cup
- ½ small onion, peeled and diced into ¼-inch pieces, about ½ cup
- 4 ounces breakfast sausage, broken into small clumps, about 1 cup
- 1 teaspoon kosher salt
- ½ teaspoon coarse black pepper
- 2 (10-inch) flour tortillas
- 4 ounces sharp cheddar cheese, grated, about 1 cup
- 4 eggs, scrambled or fried
- honey
- hot pepper sauce

1. Preheat your oven to 375°.
2. Coat the bottom of a skillet with olive oil.
3. Add the diced potatoes, pepper, onion, and sausage to the skillet and cook over medium-high heat until the potatoes are golden and the sausage is browned, about 5 to 8 minutes. Season with salt and pepper.
4. Place two tortillas on a baking sheet coated with vegetable oil spray. Place in the oven and cook for 2 to 3 minutes until crisp.
5. Cover the tortillas with half of the cheese, layer the potato-veggie mixture over the top, and then finish with the remaining cheese.
6. Put the baking sheet back into the oven and cook until the cheese melts, about 3 to 5 minutes more.
7. Drizzle with a bit of honey and a few dashes of hot pepper sauce.
8. Cut into slices and top the pizza with your choice of eggs.

Thing to Note:
The thing about the potatoes is you can use any leftover potato you have—baked, roasted, or even smashed. If you don't have any leftover potatoes, simply take a couple of small potatoes, pierce them with a fork, and place them into a microwave-safe bowl. Add a tablespoon or two of water, cover with plastic wrap, and microwave on high for several minutes to partially cook the potatoes. You want to be able to pierce them easily with a fork.

Make It "My Way":
Make your breakfast pizza unique by mixing in your favorite pizza toppings. Any pepper will do, and green onions work well. So do fresh herbs, sautéed mushrooms, and your favorite cheese. It's all good!

VIDEO: Breakfast pizza variations

Other Things with Eggs

Egg sammies are my go-to breakfast treat. This is mostly because of the existence of thin-sliced bagels and sandwich rounds. I like to use these for sammies because I prefer more things in the middle than bread on the outside, but you can certainly have your breakfast sandwich on any bread you want. Here's my favorite.

My Breakfast Sandwich
serves me
15 minutes till it's ready

- 1 thin-sliced everything bagel round, toasted
- 1 (2-ounce) breakfast sausage patty, cooked
- 1 (1-ounce) slice American cheese
- 1 Perfect Scrambled Egg
- 1 teaspoon kosher salt
- ½ teaspoon coarse black pepper

1. Lay the bottom of the bagel on your cutting board or clean work surface. Top with the sausage patty, cheese slice, and scrambled egg. Season with salt and pepper. Cover the filling with the top of the bagel.
2. The hot egg and sausage will melt the cheese and keep everything warm enough to eat right way.
3. If you have an extra couple of minutes, you can wrap the sandwich in aluminum foil, wax paper, or parchment paper and keep it warm in a warming drawer or oven set on 250°. This will allow the flavors to combine and soften the bread, making it an even better egg sandwich.

Make It "My Way":
Here goes all the combos:
- **Bacon Sammie:** Put two slices of bacon, cut in half, between a toasted English muffin. Top the bacon with a slice of cheddar cheese and a Perfect Scrambled Egg.
- **Chicken Biscuit Sammie:** Stuff a warm biscuit with one or two cooked chicken nuggets, a slice of swiss cheese, your Perfect Scrambled Egg, and a dollop of chipotle mayo.
- **Avocado Sammie:** Stack a thin-sliced sandwich round with a Perfect Scrambled Egg, slices of ripe avocado, and a few strings of pickled red onion.

Thing to Note:
It's easy to cook everything in one skillet. Start with the sausage. Smush the patty until it's thin and about ¾ the size of the bagel round. Place it into a skillet over medium heat. Cook, flipping once until it's no longer pink in the center, about 3 minutes. Use the same skillet to cook the eggs. Now, you only have one skillet to clean.

Breakfast Skillet with Glazed Eggs
serves 2
30 minutes till it's ready

- 1 to 2 tablespoons olive oil
- 4 slices bacon, diced into ½-inch pieces, about 1 cup
- 6 to 8 ounces beef, diced into ½-inch pieces, about 1 cup (I used tenderloin, but you can substitute with chunks of ham, corned beef, or chicken—it's your choice.)
- 1 medium baked potato, cooked and cut into ½-inch pieces, about 1 cup
- 1 green bell pepper, seeded and cut into ½-inch pieces, about 1 cup
- 1 white onion, peeled and cut into ½-inch pieces, about 1 cup
- 1 teaspoon kosher salt
- 1 teaspoon coarse black pepper
- 4 ounces sharp cheddar cheese, grated, about 1 cup

For eggs:
- 1 tablespoon butter
- 4 large eggs
- 2 tablespoons fresh dill, chopped

For hash:
1. Drizzle 1 tablespoon olive oil in a skillet over medium heat.
2. Add the bacon and beef. Cook until the bacon begins to crisp then remove the bacon and beef from the skillet.
3. Add the potato, pepper, and onion to the skillet. Season with salt and pepper. Cook until the onion and pepper are soft and the potato begins to brown, about 5 to 8 minutes.
4. Add the bacon and beef back on the skillet and toss. If your hash begins to stick to the skillet, you can add more oil.
5. Scatter the cheese on top of the hash. Cover the skillet and let the cheese melt, just a few minutes more.
6. Sprinkle the fresh dill over the top.

For eggs:
1. Place the butter into a sauté pan with a lid over medium heat.
2. Once the butter is melted, crack the eggs into the pan, being careful not to break the yolks, and set one half shell aside. Season eggs with salt and pepper.
3. Fill an empty eggshell half with water and pour this into the pan. The water will bubble.
4. Reduce the heat to medium-low, cover the pan with the lid, and cook the eggs until the yolks are just set (and look "glazed over"), about 3 to 4 minutes.

To finish:
1. Scoop the hash on a plate. Top the hash with eggs. Sprinkle with more fresh dill.

VIDEO: Make a glazed egg

Southern-Style Huevos Rancheros

serves 2 large or 4 small portions
30 minutes till it's ready

For baked beans:
- 1 tablespoon olive oil
- 4 slices bacon, diced into ½-inch pieces, about 1 cup
- 1 bunch (5 to 6) green onions, tough tops removed, cut into thin slices, about 1 cup
- 1 small jalapeño pepper, seeded, deveined, and finely diced, about 2 tablespoons
- 1 (16-ounce) can baked beans
- 1 teaspoon kosher salt
- ½ teaspoon coarse black pepper

For the tortilla:
- 1 tablespoon olive oil
- 2 (10-inch) spinach tortillas (you can use whichever variety of tortilla you prefer)
- 3 tablespoons butter
- 2 tablespoons Dijon-style mustard
- 2 tablespoons pure maple syrup
- 8 slices deli ham
- 4 ounces cheddar cheese, grated, about ½ cup
- 4 large eggs
- 1 avocado, pitted, peeled, and diced, about 1 cup
- 1 small tomato, diced, about ½ cup

1. Heat 1 tablespoon olive oil in a skillet over medium heat.
2. Add the bacon, onions, and jalapeño pepper and cook until the bacon begins to crisp, and the onions are soft, about 5 minutes.
3. Pour the baked beans into the skillet. Season with some of the salt and pepper. Reduce the heat to low and simmer the beans while you cook the ham.
4. Heat 1 tablespoon olive oil in a large (large enough to lay one flat tortilla in the center) skillet over medium heat.
5. When the oil is hot, carefully lay one tortilla into the oil. Cook for a few seconds. Use tongs to flip. Cook for a couple of seconds more and transfer to a large platter. Repeat with the second tortilla and transfer to a second platter.
6. Add the butter, mustard, and maple syrup to the same skillet. Stir together and melt the butter. Add the ham slices to the pan. Cook, turning occasionally, until the ham begins to brown and crisp on the edges, about 2 minutes.
7. Spoon half of the beans on one tortilla. Top the beans with half of the shredded cheese. Arrange four slices of ham on top of the cheese and beans. Repeat with the second tortilla.
8. Crack the eggs into the skillet, being careful not to break the yolks. Reduce the heat to medium-low and cook until the whites of the eggs are set, and the yolks are still runny, about 3 to 4 minutes. Season with salt and pepper.
9. Place two eggs on each tortilla. Top with diced tomatoes and avocados.

Make It "My Way":
These are two generous portions. If you are making this dish for a crowd, you can change the size of the tortilla and serve everyone a smaller portion; or if you are a fan of communal eating, serve large tortillas on an even large platter. Place it in the center of a table and pass around forks. Everyone can dig in to the same dish!

Poached Eggs in Spiced Tomato Sauce
with Olives and Feta Cheese
serves 4
30 minutes till it's ready

- 2 tablespoons olive oil
- 1 medium onion, peeled and finely diced, about 1 cup
- 2 garlic cloves, minced, about 1 tablespoon
- 1 teaspoon ground paprika
- 1 teaspoon ground cumin
- 1 teaspoon chili powder
- 1 (28-ounce can) crushed tomatoes
- 2 tablespoons tomato paste
- 1 teaspoon kosher salt
- ½ teaspoon coarse black pepper
- 4 large eggs
- 6 to 8 kalamata olives, pitted and sliced, about ¼ cup
- 3 ounces feta cheese, crumbled, about ½ cup
- 2 tablespoons fresh parsley, chopped

1. Heat the olive oil over medium heat in a sauté pan with a lid.
2. Add the onion and garlic and cook until soft, about 2 minutes.
3. Stir in the paprika, cumin, and chili powder. Cook until you smell the seasonings, about 1 minute more.
4. Pour in the tomatoes and tomato paste. Season with salt and pepper.
5. Let the sauce simmer for 5 minutes. Use a spoon to make four wells in the sauce.
6. Crack an egg into a bowl, being careful not to break the yolk, and then pour the egg into the well. Repeat with the remaining eggs. Season the eggs with salt and pepper. Cover the skillet with the lid and simmer until the eggs are set, about 3 to 4 minutes. The yolks will still jiggle a bit.
7. Top the eggs and sauce with olives, cheese, and parsley.
8. Serve the dish in the pan and use hunks of toasted bread for dipping.

VIDEO: Poaching eggs in sauce

You Can Cook Any Thing: Volume 1

Smoked Salmon Toasts
with Scallion-Caper Cream Cheese, Pickled Radishes, and Jammy Eggs
serves 4
30 minutes 'til it's ready

For pickled radishes:
- 1 bunch of radishes, about 10
- ½ cup apple cider vinegar, mixed with 1 cup warm water
- 1 tablespoon granulated sugar
- 1 ½ teaspoons kosher salt

For cream cheese:
- 4 ounces cream cheese, room temperature, about ½ cup
- 2 tablespoons sour cream
- 2 green onions, thinly sliced, about 2 tablespoons
- 2 tablespoons capers, drained

For toasts:
- 4 slices whole grain bread
- 4 ounces smoked salmon
- 4 large eggs

1. Slice the radishes into thin circles. In a bowl, stir together 1 cup warm water, cider vinegar, sugar, and salt. Add the radishes to the bowl and let them marinate for at least 30 minutes, or up to several days, in the fridge.
2. Combine the cream cheese, sour cream, green onions, and capers in a bowl.
3. Toast the bread. Spread each slice with a slather of the veggie-cream. Add slices of salmon. Remove the radishes from the liquid and place several on top of the salmon.
4. Bring water to a boil in a pot.
5. Use a spoon to place each egg into the boiling water. Boil the eggs for 6 ½ minutes.
6. Remove the eggs from the hot water and place into an ice water bath for at least 2 minutes.
7. Peel the eggs and cut in half. The centers will be just set. Slice the eggs and place them on top of the salmon. Season with salt and pepper.

VIDEO: Making a jammy egg

Chicken Liver Toasts
with Caramelized Onions and Scrambled Eggs
serves 4
30 minutes till it's ready

For onions:
- 2 tablespoons olive oil
- 2 tablespoons butter
- 2 large onions, peeled and thinly sliced, about 3 cups
- 2 tablespoons balsamic vinegar
- 1 teaspoon kosher salt
- 1 teaspoon coarse black pepper

For livers:
- 2 tablespoons olive oil
- 2 tablespoons butter
- 1 medium onion, peeled and diced, about 1 cup
- 4 large cloves garlic, minced, about 2 tablespoons
- 1 pound chicken livers
- ½ cup sherry wine

For toasts:
- 4 slices whole grain bread
- 4 Perfect Scrambled Eggs

1. Heat 2 tablespoons olive oil and 2 tablespoons butter in a large skillet over medium heat.
2. Add the 2 large, sliced onions and cook until soft and translucent, about 5 minutes.
3. Stir in the balsamic vinegar and season with salt and pepper.
4. Reduce the heat to low. Cook until the onions are golden, soft, and syrupy, about 20 minutes. Remove the skillet from the heat, cover with a lid or aluminum foil to keep the onions warm.
5. Heat 2 more tablespoons olive oil and butter in a skillet over medium-high heat.
6. Add the medium diced onion and cook until soft and golden, about 5 to 10 minutes.
7. Add the garlic and cook for 2 minutes more.
8. Add the chicken livers. Season with salt and pepper. Cook the livers for 5 minutes, stirring often.
9. Pour the sherry into the skillet. Continue cooking, using a potato masher to gently break up the livers into smaller pieces. Cook until the chicken livers are no longer pink in the center, and very little liquid remains in the skillet, about 8 to 10 minutes more. Remove the skillet from the heat, cover with a lid or aluminum foil to keep the livers warm.
10. Toast the bread. Spoon some chicken livers onto each slice. Top with caramelized onions and a spoonful of scrambled eggs.

Waffly Things

WHAT IF WE TAKE THIS SIMPLE EGG AND MIX IT INTO THINGS LIKE WAFFLE AND PANCAKE BATTER? MY OH MY ... THE POSSIBILITIES. You may think waffle and pancake batters are interchangeable, but this is not quite true! Waffles are sweeter, with a bit more fat added than pancakes. The more fat, the crispier the waffle. Here are some great waffle ideas for you to try.

Basic Waffle Batter

makes about 6 (4-inch square) waffles
15 minutes till it's ready

- 2 cups unbleached all-purpose flour
- ¼ cup granulated sugar
- 2 teaspoons baking powder
- ½ teaspoon kosher salt
- 1 ½ cups buttermilk
- 2 large eggs
- 4 tablespoons butter, ½ stick, melted
- 1 teaspoon vanilla extract

1. Preheat a waffle iron according to the manufacturer's directions.
2. Whisk together flour, sugar, baking powder, and salt in a large bowl.
3. Whisk together the buttermilk, eggs, melted butter, and vanilla extract in a smaller bowl.
4. Pour the wet ingredients into the dry ingredients and stir until just combined to create a super waffle batter ready for any of your stir-ins or is just terrific on its own.
5. Pour the batter into the waffle iron and cook until crisp on the outside and fluffy on the inside.
6. Top with fruit, maple syrup, honey, or any of your favorite things.

Thing to Note:
You can make this batter today, place it in an airtight container, and whip up the waffles up to 3 days later.

Now, let's look at ways to really enjoy those FUN waffles!

VIDEO: Making the perfect waffle

Granola Waffles
with Yogurt and Berries
makes about 6 (4-inch square) waffles
15 minutes till they're ready

- 2 cups unbleached all-purpose flour
- ¼ cup granulated sugar
- 2 teaspoons baking powder
- ½ teaspoon kosher salt
- 1 ½ cups buttermilk, room temperature
- 2 large eggs
- 4 tablespoons butter, ½ stick, melted
- 2 teaspoons vanilla extract
- ½ cup prepared granola
- yogurt (your choice)
- fresh berries
- maple syrup

1. Preheat a waffle iron according to the manufacturer's directions.
2. Whisk together flour, sugar, baking powder, and salt in a large bowl.
3. Whisk together the buttermilk, eggs, melted butter, and vanilla extract in a smaller bowl.
4. Pour the wet ingredients into the dry ingredients. Add the granola and stir everything together.
5. Pour the batter into the preheated waffle iron and cook until crisp on the outside and fluffy on the inside.
6. Top each waffle with a spoonful of yogurt, a handful of berries, and a drizzle of warm maple syrup.

Thing to Note:
To make the waffles in advance, cook them in the waffle iron and then cool to room temperature. Stack the waffles with parchment paper between each one. Place into a resealable plastic bag and freeze for up to one month. Reheat the waffles by placing on a rack in a preheated, 350° oven for 5 to 7 minutes.

Red Velvet Waffles
with Strawberry Syrup and Mascarpone Cream

makes about 6 (4-inch square) waffles
15 minutes till they're ready

For syrup:
- 2 cups maple syrup
- 1 pint fresh strawberries, stems removed, chopped, about 2 cups

For cream:
- 8 ounces mascarpone cream
- ½ cup heavy cream
- ¼ cup powdered sugar

For waffles:
- 2 cups unbleached all-purpose flour
- 3 tablespoons granulated sugar
- 1 tablespoon cocoa powder
- 2 teaspoons baking powder
- ½ teaspoon kosher salt
- 1 ½ cups buttermilk, room temperature
- 2 large eggs
- 4 tablespoons butter, melted, ½ stick
- 2 teaspoons vanilla extract
- ½ teaspoon apple cider vinegar
- several drops of natural red food coloring

1. Preheat a waffle iron according to the manufacturer's directions.
2. Pour the maple syrup into a pot over medium-high heat. Stir in the strawberries. Simmer until the strawberries are soft and begin to break down, about 5 to 7 minutes. Reduce the heat to low and keep the syrup warm.
3. Use an electric mixer to combine the mascarpone, heavy cream, and powdered sugar in a medium bowl until soft and creamy.
4. Whisk together flour, granulated sugar, cocoa powder, baking powder, and salt in a large bowl.
5. Whisk together the buttermilk, eggs, melted butter, vanilla extract, vinegar, and red food coloring in a separate bowl.
6. Pour the wet ingredients into the dry ingredients and combine.
7. Pour the batter into the waffle iron and cook until crisp on the outside and fluffy on the inside.
8. Top each waffle with dollops of cream and drizzles of syrup. Garnish with more fresh berries.

VIDEO: Making berry syrup

Cocoa Waffles
with Peanut Butter Whipped Cream and Grape Jelly Syrup
makes about 6 (4-inch square) waffles
20 minutes till they're ready

For syrup:
- 1 cup grape jelly
- 1 teaspoons corn starch mixed with 2 tablespoons water

For cream:
- 1 cup whipping cream, chilled
- 2 tablespoons creamy peanut butter
- 2 tablespoons powdered sugar

For waffles:
- 2 cups unbleached all-purpose flour
- ¼ cup granulated sugar
- ½ cup cocoa powder
- 2 teaspoons baking powder
- ½ teaspoon kosher salt
- 1 ½ cup buttermilk, room temperature
- 2 large eggs
- 4 tablespoons butter, ½ stick, melted
- 2 teaspoons vanilla extract

1. Preheat a waffle iron according to the manufacturer's directions.
2. Place the grape jelly into a pot over medium heat. When the jelly thins and is runny, about 5 minutes, stir in the cornstarch and water. Simmer over low heat until the jelly is syrupy, about 3 to 5 minutes more. Keep the syrup warm over low heat.
3. Use an electric mixer fitted with a whisk attachment to whip the cream, peanut butter, and powdered sugar in a chilled bowl until the cream gets thick and soft peaks form.
4. Whisk together flour, granulated sugar, cocoa powder, baking powder, and salt in a large bowl.
5. Whisk together the buttermilk, eggs, melted butter, and vanilla extract in a smaller bowl.
6. Pour the wet ingredients into the dry ingredients and combine.
7. Pour the batter into the waffle iron and cook until crisp on the outside and fluffy on the inside.
8. Top each waffle with a dollop of peanut butter cream and a drizzle of warm grape jelly syrup.

VIDEO: Making peanut butter whipped cream.

Lemon Sunrise Waffles
with Lemon Cream and Raspberry Syrup
makes about 6 (4-inch square) waffles
20 minutes till they're ready

For lemon cream:
- zest from 2 large lemons, about 2 tablespoons
- ½ cups granulated sugar
- 2 cups whipping cream, chilled

For raspberry syrup:
- 2 cup maples syrup
- 1 pint fresh raspberries, about 2 cups

For waffles:
- 2 cups unbleached all-purpose flour
- ¼ cup lemon-sugar (reserved from above)
- 2 teaspoons baking powder
- ½ teaspoon kosher salt
- 1 ½ cup buttermilk, room temperature
- 2 large eggs
- 4 tablespoons butter, ½ stick, melted
- 2 teaspoons vanilla extract

1. Place the lemon zest into the bowl of a food processor. Add ½ cup granulated sugar. Pulse to combine into a fine powder.
2. Reserve ¼ cup of the lemon-sugar for the waffle batter.
3. Pour the remaining lemon-sugar blend into the bowl of an electric mixer fitted with the whisk attachment. Pour in the cream and whisk until stiff peaks form.
4. Add the raspberries and maple syrup to a pot. Simmer the syrup over low heat until the raspberries begin to break down (you can help this along by using a potato masher), about 5 to 7 minutes. Strain the syrup through a colander into a bowl to remove the seeds. Return the syrup to the pot over low heat to keep warm.
5. Preheat a waffle iron according to the manufacturer's directions.
6. Whisk together flour, remaining ¼ cup lemon-sugar, baking powder and salt in a large bowl.
7. Whisk together the buttermilk, eggs, melted butter, and vanilla extract in a smaller bowl.
8. Pour the wet ingredients into the dry ingredients and combine.
9. Pour the batter into the waffle iron and cook until crisp on the outside and fluffy on the inside.
10. Top each waffle with a ladle of warm raspberry syrup and a dollop of lemon cream. Drizzle more syrup on top of the cream.

Cheddar, Bacon, and Green Onion Waffles
with Jalapeño-Maple Syrup and Glazed Eggs

makes about 6 (4-inch square) waffles
20 minutes till they're ready

For waffles:
- 2 cups unbleached all-purpose flour
- ¼ cup granulated sugar
- 2 teaspoons baking powder
- ½ teaspoon kosher salt
- 1 ½ cups buttermilk, room temperature
- 2 large eggs
- 4 tablespoons butter, ½ stick, melted
- 4 slices bacon, cooked and crumbled, about 1 cup
- 4 ounces sharp cheddar cheese, grated, about 1 cup
- 2 green onions, thinly sliced, about 2 tablespoons

For syrup:
- 2 cups maple syrup
- 1 small jalapeño pepper, seeded, deveined, and finely diced, about 2 tablespoons

For eggs:
- 1 tablespoon butter
- 4 large eggs
- ½ teaspoon coarse black pepper

1. Preheat a waffle iron according to the manufacturer's directions.
2. Whisk together flour, sugar, baking powder, and salt in a large bowl.
3. Whisk together the buttermilk, eggs, and melted butter in a smaller bowl.
4. Pour the wet ingredients into the dry ingredients and combine. Stir in the crumbled bacon, cheese, and onions.
5. Pour the maple syrup into a small pot over medium heat. Stir in the jalapeño and simmer for 5 minutes. Reduce the heat to low to keep the syrup warm.
6. Melt 1 tablespoon butter over medium heat in a sauté pan with lid.
7. Crack the eggs into the skillet, being careful not to break the yolks. Pour 1 tablespoon water around the eggs and cover with the lid. Cook until the yolks are just beginning to set and appear "glazed over," about 3 to 4 minutes. Season with salt and pepper.
8. Pour the batter into the waffle iron and cook until crisp on the outside and fluffy on the inside.
9. Top each waffle with a dousing of warm jalapeño syrup and a glazed egg on top. Garnish with more slices of green onion.

Make It "My Way":
Depending on your palate's spice tolerance, feel free to use more or less jalapeño in the syrup. During the summer, you'll find all sorts of varieties of peppers in the market. Experimenting is much of the fun, and this recipe is just perfect for it. Substituting with other cheeses and proteins is also fun. How 'bout a combination of Parmesan and prosciutto, or goat cheese and country ham, or Fontina cheese and sausage? Oh, I can go on and on ....

Buttermilk Biscuit Waffles
with Sausage Gravy
makes about 6 (4-inch square) waffles
20 minutes till they're ready

For gravy:
- 1 pound pork sausage
- 6 tablespoons butter, ¾ stick
- 1 small onion, peeled and diced, about ½ cup
- 2 cloves garlic, minced, about 1 tablespoon
- 6 tablespoons unbleached all-purpose flour
- 1 ½ cups chicken stock
- 1 ½ cups whole milk
- 1 teaspoon kosher salt
- ½ teaspoon coarse black pepper
- ½ teaspoon dried thyme
- ¼ teaspoon ground allspice

For waffles:
- 2 cups unbleached all-purpose flour
- 1 tablespoon baking powder
- ½ teaspoon kosher salt
- ½ teaspoon dried thyme
- 6 tablespoons butter, cold, cut into small pieces, ¾ stick
- 1 ½ cups buttermilk, room temperature
- 1 large egg, beaten
- 1 tablespoon chopped fresh chives

1. Preheat a waffle iron according to the manufacturer's directions.
2. Cook the sausage in a skillet over medium-high heat, breaking up the clumps into small pieces, until well-browned, about 5 to 7 minutes.
3. Transfer the sausage to a plate, keeping the fat in the skillet.
4. Add 1 tablespoon of butter to the skillet and melt.
5. Add the onion and garlic and cook until the veggies are soft and fragrant, about 3 to 5 minutes.
6. Reduce the heat to medium and melt 5 more tablespoons butter with the onion and garlic.
7. Whisk in the flour. Stir until the mixture is smooth and bubbling. Whisk in the stock and continue to stir until the gravy begins to thicken. Whisk in the milk. Season with salt, pepper, thyme, and allspice.
8. Stir the sausage back into the gravy. Reduce the heat to low to keep the gravy warm.
9. Place the flour, baking powder, and salt in a bowl. Add the butter.
10. Use a pastry cutter or two forks to cut 6 tablespoons chilled butter into the flour to form a mixture of coarse crumbs. You want the flour to look like it is made up of little "pea-sized" clumps.
11. Stir in the buttermilk and egg. The batter will be thicker than waffle batter but not as dense as biscuit dough.
12. Spoon the batter into the waffle iron and cook until crisp on the outside and fluffy on the inside.
13. Serve the waffles topped with a ladleful of sausage gravy and garnished with chopped chives.

You Can Cook Any Thing: Volume 1

Pancakey Things

SHALL I COMPARE THEE TO A SUMMER'S DAY? AND SHALL I COMPARE THE SUN RISING IN THE SKY TO THE PANCAKE BLOSSOMING ON MY GRIDDLE? Perhaps not, but I can talk about the dawning smiles on little ones' faces when they come to the morning table to find those hot cakes coming off the griddle.

It is a great idea to bank a box or two of prepared pancake mix in your pantry. But it's easy for you to make your own mix in a pinch. The things that make pancakes so much fun are the add-ins and add-ons. My family favs are tossing in a few chocolate chips or berries, and dousing the cakes in melted butter and fruity syrup. We can get even more creative sometimes. Just check out a couple of these ideas!

"My Way" Pancakes
serves 4 to 6
25 minutes till they're ready

For "My Way" pancake mix:
- 2 cups unbleached all-purpose flour
- ¼ cup granulated sugar
- 4 teaspoons baking powder
- ¼ teaspoon baking soda
- ½ teaspoon kosher salt

For pancakes:
- 1 ¾ cups whole milk
- 1 large egg
- 4 tablespoons butter, melted, plus 1 more for the skillet and more for topping
- 1 teaspoon vanilla
- maple syrup

1. Whisk the pancake mix ingredients together in a large bowl.
2. Whisk the milk, egg, melted butter, and vanilla in a separate bowl until smooth.
3. Make a well in the center of the dry ingredients. Whisk the wet ingredients into the dry ingredients until the batter is just smooth. Having a couple of lumps in the batter is just fine!
4. Heat a griddle over medium-high heat. (You can also use a large, non-stick skillet.) Reduce the heat to low and melt a tablespoon of butter on the grill. Use a paper towel to wipe off the excess so there is a sheer coating of butter.
5. Ladle about ¼ to ½ cup of batter on the grill. Cook until bubbles form on the top of the cake, and the bottom is golden brown, about 3 minutes. Flip and cook on the other side, about 3 minutes more.
6. Serve with melted butter and warm maple syrup.

Make It "My Way":
Here's where it gets fun. After you ladle the batter onto the griddle, you can add your favorite things to your pancakes. Mini chocolate chips; blueberries; or other fruits, nuts, sprinkles, and spices like cinnamon and ginger are just a couple of ideas. You can also drizzle your baked cakes with your favorite syrup, honey, or glaze.

VIDEO: Making blueberry pancakes

You Can Cook Any Thing: Volume 1

Cinnamon-Apple Pancakes
serves 4 to 6
30 minutes till they're ready

- 2 cups "My Way" pancake mix
- 1 teaspoon ground cinnamon
- 1 teaspoon ground ginger
- ½ teaspoon ground nutmeg
- 1 ¾ cups whole milk
- 1 large egg
- 4 tablespoons butter, melted, plus 1 tablespoon more for the grill
- 1 teaspoon vanilla
- 1 medium apple, peeled and grated, about 1 cup

1. Whisk the pancake mix ingredients together in a large bowl. Add the cinnamon, ginger, and nutmeg.
2. Whisk the milk, egg, melted butter, vanilla, and grated apple in a separate bowl until smooth.
3. Make a well in the center of the dry ingredients. Whisk the wet ingredients into the dry ingredients until the batter is just smooth. A couple of lumps are nothing to worry about.
4. Heat a griddle over medium-high heat. (You can also use a large, non-stick skillet.) Reduce the heat to low and melt a tablespoon of butter on the grill. Use a paper towel to wipe off the excess so there is a sheer coating of butter.
5. Ladle about ¼ to ½ cup batter onto the grill. Cook until bubbles form on the top of the cake, and the bottom is golden brown, about 3 minutes. Flip and cook on the other side, about 3 minutes more.
6. Serve with melted butter and warm maple syrup.

Princess Pancakes
serves 4 to 6
30 minutes till they're ready

For glaze:
- 1 cup heavy cream
- ½ cup maple syrup
- 4 ounces cream cheese, cut into chunks, about ½ cup
- 1 tablespoon vanilla
- ⅛ teaspoon kosher salt

For pancakes:
- 2 cups "My Way" pancake mix
- 2 tablespoons sprinkles
- 1 ¾ cups whole milk
- 1 large egg
- 4 tablespoons butter, melted, plus 1 tablespoon more for the grill
- 1 teaspoon vanilla

1. Heat the cream in a deep pot over medium heat. Add the maple syrup, cream cheese, and vanilla. Season with a bit of salt to cut the sweetness. Stir until the mixture is smooth and just beginning to bubble, about 5 minutes. Remove from the heat and keep warm.
2. Whisk together the pancake mix ingredients in a large bowl. Add the sprinkles.
3. Whisk the milk, egg, melted butter, and vanilla in a separate bowl until smooth.
4. Make a well in the center of the dry ingredients. Whisk the wet ingredients into the dry ingredients until the batter is just smooth. A few lumps aren't a problem.
5. Heat a griddle over medium-high heat. Reduce the heat to low and melt a tablespoon of butter on the grill. Use a paper towel to wipe off the excess so there is a sheer coating of butter.
6. Ladle about ¼ to ½ cup batter on the grill. Cook until bubbles form on the top of the cake, and the bottom is golden brown, about 3 minutes. Flip and cook on the other side, about 3 minutes more.
7. Pile several pancakes on a plate. Spoon the warm glaze over the top. Scatter more sprinkles all over.

Pumpkin Pie Pancakes
with Sugared Pecans
serves 4 to 6
30 minutes till it's ready

Make It "My Way":
These pumpkin pie pancakes will taste even better with a dollop of whipped cream!

Thing to Note:
You can buy your pumpkin pie spice in the grocery store or make your own. Mix 3 tablespoons ground cinnamon, 1 tablespoon ground ginger, 2 teaspoons ground nutmeg, 1½ teaspoons ground allspice, and 1 teaspoon ground cloves. Store in a small, airtight jar for up to several months.

For topping:
- 2 tablespoons butter
- 2 tablespoons brown sugar
- 1 teaspoon pumpkin pie spice
- 4 ounces pecans, chopped, about ¾ cup
- ⅛ teaspoon kosher salt

For pancakes:
- 2 cups "My Way" pancake mix
- 2 tablespoons pumpkin pie spice
- 1 ¾ cups whole milk
- 1 large egg
- 1 teaspoon vanilla
- 4 tablespoons butter, melted, plus 1 tablespoon more for the grill
- maple syrup

1. Melt 2 tablespoons butter in a skillet over medium heat. Stir in the brown sugar and pumpkin pie spice. When the mixture is melted and bubbly, stir in the pecans. Season with a bit of salt to cut the sweetness. Cook until the nuts are coated with sauce and fragrant, about 3 to 4 minutes. Turn off the heat.
2. Whisk together the pancake mix ingredients and pumpkin pie spice in a large bowl.
3. Whisk the milk, eggs, melted butter, and vanilla in a separate bowl until smooth.
4. Make a well in the center of the dry ingredients. Whisk the wet ingredients into the dry ingredients until the batter is just smooth. A couple of lumps are nothing to worry about.
5. Heat a griddle over medium-high heat. Reduce the heat to low and melt a tablespoon of butter on the grill. Use a paper towel to wipe off the excess so there is a sheer coating of butter.
6. Ladle about ¼ to ½ cup batter on the grill. Cook until bubbles form on the top of the cake, and the bottom is golden brown, about 3 minutes. Flip and cook on the other side, about 3 minutes more.
7. Serve the pancakes with a spoonful of sugared pecans and a drizzle of warm maple syrup.

Buckwheat Flapjacks
with Sausage and Maple Syrup
serves 4 to 6
40 minutes till they're ready

- 1 ½ cups buckwheat flour
- ½ cup unbleached all-purpose flour
- 1 tablespoon granulated sugar
- 1 teaspoon baking powder
- ½ teaspoon baking soda
- ½ teaspoons kosher salt
- 2 cups buttermilk
- 2 large eggs
- 4 tablespoons butter, melted, plus 1 more for the skillet and more for topping
- 1 teaspoon vanilla
- ½ pound pork sausage
- 1 tablespoon olive oil
- maple syrup

1. Whisk together the flours, sugar, baking powder, soda, and salt in a bowl.
2. Whisk the buttermilk, eggs, melted butter, and vanilla in a separate bowl until smooth.
3. Make a well in the center of the dry ingredients. Whisk the wet ingredients into the dry ingredients until the batter is just smooth.
4. Form the sausage into palm-size patties. Flatten to about ½-inch thick. Heat olive oil in a skillet over medium heat. Add the patties and cook until golden on one side, about 3 minutes. Flip, flatten a bit more with your spatula, and cook until the sausage is no longer pink in the center, about 3 minutes more.
5. Heat a griddle over medium-high heat. Reduce the heat to low and melt a tablespoon of butter on the grill. Use a paper towel to wipe off the excess so there is a sheer coating of butter.
6. Ladle about ¾ cup batter on the grill, covering the entire bottom of the 10-inch pan. Cook until bubbles form on the top of the cake, and the bottom is golden brown, about 3 minutes. Flip and cook on the other side, about 3 minutes more.
7. Serve the flapjacks with a pat of butter, a sausage patty (or two), and a drizzle of warmed maple syrup over everything.

Make It "My Way":
Flapjacks are called flapjacks because they are bigger and thicker than traditional pancakes and "flap" as you flip 'em! To make these authentic, cook them in a 10-inch skillet and let the batter totally cover the bottom. You'll need a couple of spatulas to flip over the flapjack, and you'll need to cook it longer than a pancake. But it's well worth the effort!

Cheesy Things

IF IT WERE UP TO ME, CHEESE WOULD BE ITS OWN FOOD GROUP. I love all kinds of cheese. I love cheese boards, cheese and crackers, cheese and fruit plates, squares of cheese for snacks, slices of cheese on sandwiches, melted cheese on casseroles, globs of cheese on pizza, chunks of cheese in salads, and, most of all, my all-time favorite ... grilled cheese sandwiches!

I think if you asked any American what their favorite comfort fast-food is, the answer would be a grilled cheese sandwich. What could be better than melty cheese oozing out of perfectly crisp, toasted bread? Nothing! A grilled cheese is a quick and inexpensive meal. But it can also elevate to one spectacular sandwich. Let's take a look.

"My Way" Basic Grilled Cheese Sandwich

serves 1
5 minutes till it's ready

- 2 tablespoons butter
- 2 slices bread (your choice)
- 2 to 4 (1-ounce) slices cheese (your choice)
- 2 tablespoons mayonnaise

1. Melt the butter in a sauté pan over medium-high heat.
2. Place the cheese in between the bread slices.
3. Now this is where it gets FUN. Spread the outsides of each sandwich with mayonnaise. Yes, it's more common to use butter, but mayo will serve the same purpose in giving your sandwich the perfect golden crunch.
4. Place the sandwich into the pan. Cook for 30 seconds then flip. This first 30 seconds makes sure the top side of the bread will crisp.
5. Reduce the heat to medium and cook until the underside is golden, about 2 minutes more.
6. Flip one last time and cover the sandwich with the lid of the pan or a piece of aluminum foil.
7. Cook until the cheese is melted, and the underside is golden-brown.
8. Transfer the sandwich to a plate. Keep the sandwich covered for 30 seconds while the cheese settles down, and then you are ready to eat!

VIDEO: Making the perfect grilled cheese sandwich

Thing to Note:
If you want to keep things simple, plain white sandwich bread and American cheese are the standard for this sandwich. While this is a great start, the possibilities are endless for grilled cheese. Here are some good combos:

- **All American Grilled Cheese:** turkey, avocado, sliced tomato, and white Vermont cheddar
- **Breakfast Grilled Cheese:** thick sliced ham, scrambled eggs, and gruyère
- **Apple Pie Grilled Cheese:** bacon, sliced apples, and cheddar cheese
- **Pizza Grilled Cheese:** pepperoni, sun-dried tomatoes, basil, and mozzarella cheese
- **Sunday Night Grilled Cheese:** leftover meatloaf, caramelized onions, and brie cheese
- **Philly Steak Grilled Cheese:** thinly sliced beef, sautéed bell peppers and onions, and provolone cheese
- **My Mac Grilled Cheese:** a spoonful of mac and cheese and layers of cheddar cheese
- **Buffalo Grilled Cheese:** buffalo spiced chicken, blue cheese dressing, and chopped celery

I can go on and on, but let's stop there for now. Let's take this sandwich to the next level!

"My Way" Tuna Melt
with Pickled Vegetables
serves 6
30 minutes till it's ready

For pickled veg:
- 3 radishes, thinly sliced, about ½ cup
- 1 carrot, peeled and thinly sliced, about ½ cup
- 1 small red onion, thinly sliced, about ½ cup
- 1 mini cucumber, thinly sliced, about ½ cup
- ½ cup white wine vinegar
- 1 tablespoon honey
- ½ teaspoon kosher salt
- ½ teaspoon coarse black pepper

For tuna salad:
- 1 (6-ounce) can tuna packed in oil, drained
- 1 celery rib, diced, about ½ cup
- ¼ cup mayonnaise
- 4 to 6 cornichons, finely diced, about 2 tablespoons
- juice of ½ large lemon, about 1 tablespoon
- 1 tablespoon fresh parsley, finely chopped

For melts:
- 3 English muffins, split
- 2 tablespoons mayonnaise
- 1 medium tomato, cut into 6 thin slices
- 4 ounce sharp cheddar cheese, grated, about 1 cup

For pickled veg:
1. Place the veggies into a bowl. Pour in the vinegar. Stir in the honey and ¼ cup warm water. Season with salt and pepper.
2. Let the veggies sit in the liquid for 20 minutes and up to a couple of days in the fridge. To serve, drain the veggies from the liquid.

For melts:
1. In a separate bowl, use a fork to break up the tuna into small pieces.
2. Mix in the celery, mayo, cornichons, lemon juice, and parsley. Season with salt and pepper.
3. Crisp the muffins in a toaster and place them cut side up on your work surface. Spread each one with mayonnaise. Layer a tomato slice on top of the mayo. Spread tuna salad on top of the tomato. You will have six open-faced sandwiches.
4. Transfer the muffins to a baking sheet lined with parchment paper.
5. Sprinkle the cheese on top of the tuna.
6. Turn your oven to broil.
7. Place the baking sheet into the oven and broil until the cheese is melted and bubbling.
8. Remove the baking sheet from the oven and serve the tuna melts warm with pickled veggies on top.

Thing to Note:
Broiling is a great way to get a thing really hot, really quickly. The secret to avoiding burnt food is to watch it carefully while it's cooking. Place the top rack close to the top broiling element in your oven. Make sure you have room between the top of your pan and the bottom of the broiler. You might need to have the rack set one space below the top setting. Place the baking sheet under the broiler and watch as the cheese bubbles.

Another Thing to Note:
Cornichons are tiny, tart, French pickles. You most often see them on charcuterie boards. They add a punch of pickly flavor to this and many other salads.

Open-Faced Cheese-Topped Sloppy Joes

serves 8
30 minutes till it's ready

- 2 tablespoons olive oil
- 2 pounds ground sirloin beef
- 1/3 cup brown sugar
- 2 tablespoons prepared steak seasoning
- 1 large yellow onion, peeled and diced, about 1 cup
- 1 red bell pepper, seeded and chopped, about ½ cup
- 2 cups marinara sauce
- 2 tablespoons tomato paste
- 1 teaspoon kosher salt
- ½ teaspoon coarse black pepper
- 8 burger buns
- 4 ounces cheddar cheese, shredded, about 1 cup

1. Heat the olive oil in a skillet over medium-high heat.
2. Add the beef and cook, breaking the chunks into small pieces, until browned, about 6 to 10 minutes. Add the brown sugar, steak seasoning, onion, and pepper. Cook for 5 minutes more.
3. Reduce the heat to medium.
4. Stir in marinara sauce and tomato paste. Simmer for 15 minutes. Season with salt and pepper.
5. Turn your oven to the broil setting. Place the buns on a baking sheet. Spoon the sloppy joe mixture on the buns and top with cheese.
6. Place the baking sheet in the oven for 2 to 4 minutes or until the cheese has melted.

Thing to Note:
Don't have a jar of marinara sauce? It doesn't take long to make your own. Chop some onion, carrots, and garlic and sauté them in olive oil for a couple of minutes until everything is soft. Add a 28-ounce can crushed tomatoes, 2 tablespoons tomato paste, 1 teaspoon granulated sugar, and 1 teaspoon dried oregano. Stir and simmer until everything comes together, and the kitchen smells really good. Season with salt and pepper. Just like that—you've got sauce!

Pimento Cheese Things

Other than delicious, what is pimento cheese? Basically, it's a mixture of cheeses you can use for any recipes that call for cheese. It is its own thing but can be used as a condiment or spread. Making pimento cheese is all about using whatever cheese and spices you have on hand and adding a good amount of diced pimentos, which are heart-shaped peppers with more sweet than heat. Let me show you what I mean.

Here is my recipe for classic pimento cheese. But this is also an invitation for you to create your favorite blend of spices and cheeses to make a spread that knocks your socks off!

Pimento Cheese
makes about 2 cups
10 minutes till it's ready

- 4 ounces sharp cheddar cheese, grated, about 1 cup
- 4 ounces cream cheese, room temperature, about ½ cup
- 2 green onions, thinly sliced, about 2 tablespoons
- 3 tablespoons mayonnaise
- ½ teaspoon onion powder
- ½ teaspoon garlic powder
- ¼ teaspoon paprika
- 1 (4-ounce) jar chopped pimentos, drained
- ½ teaspoon kosher salt
- ½ teaspoon coarse black pepper

1. Place the cheddar cheese, cream cheese, green onions, mayo, onion powder, garlic powder, and paprika in the bowl of a food processor. Pulse to combine. Add the pimentos and season with salt and pepper. Pulse a few more times.

Let's put this all together and create a few of my absolute most favorite cheese sandwiches.

VIDEO: Making your favorite pimento cheese

Thing to Note:
This is a traditional recipe for pimento cheese. However, your pimento cheese is yours! Feel free to swap out the cheese for whatever you have on hand. In place of cheddar, substitute Monterey Jack, American, Gouda, Swiss, gruyere or a combination all these. Pimento is great, but you can substitute with roasted red pepper, sun-dried tomatoes, or Peppadew peppers. I sometimes add diced jalapeño or poblano peppers. For a creamier version, I add a spoonful of sour cream or unflavored greek yogurt. Do what feels right to you—you can't mess this up!

Best Grilled Cheese Sammy Evah!

makes 2 yummy sandwiches
30 minutes till it's ready

- 4 slices bread, thickly sliced
- 1 cup pimento cheese
- 4 (1-ounce) slices swiss cheese
- 4 to 6 strips cooked bacon
- 4 (1-ounce) slices cheddar cheese
- 2 to 3 tablespoons fruit jam
- 2 to 3 tablespoons mayonnaise
- 2 tablespoons butter

1. Lay the bread slices on your work surface. Spread each slice with pimento cheese. Top two slices with swiss cheese first then bacon and cheddar. Dollop jam on the other two slices. Close the sandwiches.
2. Spread mayonnaise on both sides of the sandwich.
3. Heat the butter in a skillet over medium-high heat until it melts and is foamy.
4. Place the sandwiches into the melted butter. Let cook for 30 seconds then flip and reduce the heat to medium. Cook until the underside is golden-brown, about 3 to 4 minutes. Flip the sandwich once more to cook the second side to golden, about 2 minutes more.
5. Turn off the heat. Check to see if your cheese is melted enough. If not, cover the sandwiches with foil for a minute or two before serving.
6. Transfer the sandwiches to your work surface and cut in half. (You can cut them in fourths if you are sharing.)

Thing to Note:
Any fruit jam will do for this recipe. We want just a hint of sweetness to compliment all that savory cheese. You can substitute with chutney or honey. If you are missing jam but have a few extra berries laying around in your fridge, simply place them in a pot with a bit of sugar and cook them down over medium heat to make your own.

VIDEO: Making chutney

You Can Cook Any Thing: Volume 1

Pimento Cheese Sandwiches
with Fried Bologna
makes 4 sandwiches
30 minutes till it's ready

- 2 tablespoons butter
- 8 slices bologna
- 8 slices bread, thickly sliced and toasted
- 1 ½ to 2 cups pimento cheese
- dill pickle chips
- potato chips

1. Melt the butter in a skillet over medium heat.
2. Add the bologna and cook, turning once or twice until the slices are golden-brown and have crispy burnt edges, about 2 to 3 minutes. Transfer to a platter.
3. Lay the toasted bread slices on your work surface. Spread pimento cheese on each slice. Layer with bologna, pickles, and chips. Close the sandwiches and smoosh down to crunch those chips. Cut in half and dig in!

Pimento Cheese Apps

Pimento cheese can also create fantabulous apps and sides. Here are a couple for you to sample.

I call these "crack" crackers because they're just so unbelievably addicting.

Chili-Spiced Pimento Cheese
with Crack Crackers
serves a crowd
30 minutes till it's ready

For seasoned crackers:
- 1 sleeve soda crackers (also called saltines)
- 1 teaspoon garlic powder
- 1 teaspoon onion powder
- ½ teaspoon dried chili powder
- ½ teaspoon dried cilantro
- 6 tablespoons butter, melted

For pimento cheese:
- 4 ounces Monterrey Jack cheese, grated, about 1 cup
- 4 ounces cream cheese, room temperature, about ½ cup
- ¼ small red onion, peeled and diced, about 2 tablespoons
- 1 small jalapeño pepper, seeded, deveined, and diced, about 2 tablespoons
- 3 tablespoons mayonnaise
- ½ teaspoon onion powder
- ½ teaspoon garlic powder
- ½ teaspoon chili powder
- 1 small red bell pepper, charred, peeled, and diced, about ¼ cup
- 2 tablespoons fresh cilantro, chopped
- ½ teaspoon kosher salt
- ½ teaspoon coarse black pepper

For seasoned crackers:
1. Preheat your oven to 375°.
2. Lay the crackers on a baking sheet.
3. Stir the seasonings into the melted butter.
4. Brush each cracker with the seasoned butter.
5. Bake until the crackers are golden-brown, about 5 to 8 minutes.
6. Remove from the oven and cool to room temperature. The crackers can be stored in an airtight container for several days.

For pimento cheese:
1. Place the Monterrey Jack cheese, cream cheese, red onion, jalapeño, mayo, onion powder, garlic powder, and chili powder in the bowl of a food processor. Pulse to combine.
2. Add the charred pepper and cilantro and season with salt and pepper. Pulse once more.
3. Serve the crackers with a slather of pimento cheese on the top for an open-faced cheese sandwich snack.

VIDEO: Making seasoned crackers

Pimento Cheese Deviled Eggs

makes 12 deviled eggs
30 minutes till it's ready

- 6 large eggs
- 2 tablespoons mayonnaise
- 2 to 3 tablespoons pimento cheese
- 1 to 2 tablespoons sour cream
- ½ teaspoon kosher salt
- ½ teaspoon coarse black pepper

1. Arrange the eggs in a single layer in the bottom of a pot with lid. Cover with cold water. Place the lid on the pot and bring to a boil.
2. Once the water starts boiling, turn off the heat and let sit for 11 minutes.
3. Remove the lid and place the eggs in cold water. When the eggs are completely cool, peel each one.
4. Cut each egg, horizontally, into halves. Place the egg halves on an egg platter.
5. Carefully remove the yolks with a spoon and place them into a food processor. Add the mayonnaise, pimento cheese, and sour cream. Pulse to combine.
6. If the mixture is too thick, add more sour cream. If it is too thin, add more pimento cheese!
7. Taste and season with salt and pepper.
8. Fill a resealable plastic bag with the cheese-yolk filling. Use your hands to wring the bag and push the filling into the bottom corner. Twist the air out of the bag. Snip off the corner and pipe the filling into the egg halves.

VIDEO: Making a jammy egg

Pimento Cheese Pin Wheels
with Turkey, Ham, and Asparagus Spears

makes a whole bunch
30 minutes till it's ready

- ½ pound deli ham, sliced medium (or sandwich sliced)
- ½ pound deli turkey, sliced medium (or sandwich sliced)
- 1 pound fresh asparagus, trimmed and blanched
- 2 red bell peppers, roasted, charred skin peeled, sliced into strips, about 1 ½ cups
- 2 cups pimento cheese

1. Lay a slice of ham or turkey on your work surface. The meat should be thick enough to spread with pimento cheese without splitting. If the meat you have is thinner than this, layer two slices together.
2. Spread pimento cheese over the ham slice.
3. Place either half an asparagus spear or a slice of roasted pepper on the bottom end of the slathered ham slice and then roll it up!
4. Use a sharp knife to cut the roll into ½-inch slices.

There you have it ... a pimento cheese pin wheel. Bet you can't eat just one!

Thing to Note:
You can also wrap your cheese in a soft tortilla. Lay the tortilla on your work surface. Spread with cheese. Top with slices of ham or turkey and layer with asparagus and thin slices of red pepper. Wrap it all up and slice into pinwheels.

Panini Sandwiches

Paninis are a great way to take grilled cheese to gourmet sandwich status. You can put anything and everything into a panini. Roasted veggies, beef, pork, and chicken; sauces and condiments; and of course ... cheese. A great panini can be created from last night's meal. Leftover meatloaf topped with grilled onions, fresh spinach leaves, russian dressing, and crumbled blue cheese is one of my best creations.

Here are some other ideas.

Cobb Panini
makes 2 sandwiches
30 minutes till it's ready

- ½ pound bacon
- 4 thick slices whole grain bread
- 2 to 3 tablespoons olive oil
- 2 tablespoons mayonnaise
- 6 ounces blue cheese, crumbled, about 1 cup
- 1 avocado, pitted, peeled, and sliced, about 1 cup
- 1 boneless chicken breast, halved, roasted, sliced, about 1 cup
- 1 large egg, cooked, peeled, and sliced
- 1 large tomato, cored and sliced
- 1 teaspoon kosher salt
- 1 teaspoon coarse black pepper
- 1 tablespoon Dijon-style mustard

1. Cook the bacon in a skillet over medium heat. Remove the bacon and lay it on a couple of paper towels to drain the excess grease.
2. Preheat a panini press. (If you do not have one, you can use a grill pan with a weighted skillet on top of the sandwiches.)
3. Brush one side of each bread slice with olive oil.
4. Lay two pieces of bread on your work surface, oil side down. Spread mayonnaise over both slices of bread. Layer with slices of bacon, half of the blue cheese, and then the avocado slices, roasted chicken slices, sliced egg, and tomato slices. Season with salt and pepper and top with the remaining blue cheese.
5. Spread mustard on the non-oiled side of the remaining two bread slices and close the sandwiches.
6. Carefully transfer the sandwiches to the panini press. Press the top of the panini grill on the sandwiches. Increase the pressure to gently flatten the sandwiches.
7. Cook until the cheese melts, and the bread is golden, about 5 to 7 minutes.
8. Cut the panini in half and serve warm.

Avocado and Gruyere Panini
with Olive Tapenade
makes 4 sandwiches
30 minutes till it's ready

For tapenade:
- 2 to 3 medium anchovies
- 1 garlic clove, peeled
- zest from 1 large lemon, about 1 tablespoon
- juice from 1 large lemon, about 3 tablespoons
- 10 to 12 Niçoise olives, pitted
- 1 tablespoon capers, rinsed
- 2 tablespoons fresh basil, chopped
- ¼ cup olive oil
- ½ teaspoon kosher salt
- ½ teaspoon coarse black pepper

For panini:
- 8 thick slices sourdough bread
- 8 ounces gruyere cheese, grated, about 2 cups
- 2 large avocados, pitted, peeled, and sliced, about 2 cups
- 1 (7-ounce) jar sun-dried tomatoes in oil, drained, sliced lengthwise into strips
- 1 bunch watercress, washed, dried, stems removed, about 2 cups

Preheat a panini press.

For tapenade:
1. Place anchovy fillets, garlic, lemon zest and juice, olives, capers, and basil into a food processor. Pulse to combine.
2. With the machine running, slowly pour in olive oil until smooth.
3. Season with salt and freshly ground pepper.
4. Store tapenade in an airtight container in the refrigerator for up to two weeks.

For sandwiches:
1. Lay the bread slices on a cutting board. Spread each slice with tapenade.
2. Cover four of the bread slices with the cheese. Layer each with avocado, sun-dried tomato, and watercress. Cover with the remaining four bread slices, tapenade side down.
3. Place the sandwiches into the panini press and close the top to smash the sandwich together.
4. Cook until the bread is golden, and the cheese is melting, about 6 to 8 minutes.

Pepperoni Pizza Panini

makes 4 sandwiches
30 minutes till it's ready

For cheese:
- 8 ounces ricotta cheese, about 2 cups
- 1 large egg
- 2 ounces Parmesan cheese, grated, about ½ cup
- 2 tablespoons fresh, chopped basil
- ½ teaspoon dried oregano
- ½ teaspoon onion powder
- ½ teaspoon garlic powder
- 1 teaspoon kosher salt
- ½ teaspoon coarse black pepper

For panini:
- 8 slices thick, crusty bread, (sour dough, ciabatta, multigrain—you pick!)
- 2 to 4 tablespoons olive oil
- 8 ounces mozzarella cheese, grated, about 2 cups
- 8 ounces pepperoni, sliced, about 1 cup
- 1 bell pepper, seeded and deveined, diced, about 1 cup
- 1 small onion, peeled and diced, about 1 cup
- 1 cup marinara sauce

Preheat a panini press.

For cheese:
1. Place the ricotta cheese, egg, Parmesan cheese, basil, oregano, and onion and garlic powders into a bowl. Whisk together. Season with salt and pepper.

For sandwiches:
1. Lay the bread slices on your work surface. Spread each with olive oil and place olive oil side down.
2. Spread each slice with the ricotta mixture and pile on mozzarella.
3. Layer four slices with pepperoni, bell pepper, and onion. Drizzle a bit of marinara sauce over the top.
4. Top with the remaining bread slices, cheese side down.
5. Place two sandwiches at a time into the panini press. Slide the cover down and press to smash the sandwiches together.
6. Grill until golden on both sides with the cheese melted.

Make It "My Way":
Make this panini even more pizza-like by topping the sandwich with a couple of extra slices of pepperoni. Or better yet, layer two panini on top of each other and smash again. So many combinations ... yum!

Brisket Panini
on Texas Toasts
makes 2 sandwiches
30 minutes till it's ready

For toasts:
- 4 thick slices bread
- ½ cup butter, 1 stick, melted
- 1 tablespoon garlic powder
- 1 teaspoon dried oregano
- ½ teaspoon kosher salt

For sandwiches:
- ¼ cup barbecue sauce
- 4 ounces sharp cheddar cheese, shredded, about 1 cup
- ½ pound smoked brisket, thinly sliced or chopped
- dill pickle slices
- 2 tablespoons mayonnaise

For toasts:
1. Preheat oven to 375°.
2. Lay the bread on a baking sheet.
3. Mix melted butter, garlic powder, oregano, and salt in a small bowl. Brush the butter mixture on both sides of bread.
4. Bake until the top of the bread is golden and toasty, about 3 to 5 minutes. Remove the baking sheet from the oven and flip the bread over. Bake until the top side is golden and toasty, about 3 to 5 minutes more.

For the sandwiches:
1. Preheat a panini press.
2. Spread all four slices of toast with barbecue sauce.
3. Add half of the cheese on top two slices and add the brisket. Add pickles and the rest of the cheese. Top the sandwiches with the last two toasts.
4. Spread mayo on the outside of the sandwiches.
5. Place these into the panini press and lower the top to mush everything together.
6. Cook until the cheese is melted, just a couple of minutes.

Noodly Things

MACARONI NOODLES AND CHEESE … who doesn't love it? Of course, everyone has preferences. Maybe it's a baked casserole, hot from the oven with a buttery breadcrumb crust that cracks with the first scoop. Perhaps yours has no crust but is chock-full of gooey, stringy cheese. Or perhaps, your favorite are shells stirred into a cheddar-cream sauce. Any way you like it, you can make mac and cheese your way in just a couple of steps.

The Noodles

For really great mac and cheese, you want pasta shapes that can really soak up the sauce. Elbows are traditional, but mini penne, shell, and orecchiette pasta shapes work just as well.

The secret to perfect pasta is to cook it properly. Bring a pot of water to a boil. Add a palmful of salt. It will bubble at this point, so be careful. Add the pasta and continue to cook until the noodles are soft. Use a colander to drain the pasta.

If you are baking the noodles, you'll want to taste one to make sure they are just a tad underdone because the noodles will continue to bake in the casserole.

If you are stirring the noodles into the sauce, cook them until soft (but not mushy). For dried pasta, this will take between 10 and 12 minutes. For fresh pasta, only a couple of minutes.

That's it for "Noodles 101." Let's make some sauce.

White Sauce

I'm not sure if it was thanks to the charm of my surroundings, but I had the absolute best mac and cheese I ever ate in Northern Italy. The elbows were small and perfectly tender. Each noodle held its shape in the sauce, so you knew they were perfectly cooked. A delicate, creamy white sauce with just a hint of nutmeg lightly coated the pasta. Parmesan cheese shavings and a grind of fresh pepper finished the dish. Amazing!

It was the sauce that made the dish spectacular and so different from what you'd find in the United States. This basic sauce is the foundation for all great mac and cheese dishes, and it goes like this:

White Sauce for Mac and Cheese

makes about 2 cups
15 minutes till it's ready

- 4 tablespoons butter, ½ stick
- ¼ cup unbleached all-purpose flour
- 2 cups whole milk
- ½ teaspoon kosher salt
- ¼ teaspoon white pepper
- ⅛ teaspoon ground nutmeg
- 2 ounces Parmesan cheese, grated, about ½ cup

1. Melt the butter in a pot over medium heat.
2. Once the butter melts and starts to bubble, whisk in the flour. Cook the flour in the butter, whisking it around on the bottom of the pot to produce a smooth paste (a roux), about 1 to 2 minutes.
3. Slowly pour the milk into the paste, whisking until combined.
4. Reduce the heat to medium-low and continue cooking and whisking until the sauce begins to thicken. You will know the sauce is thick enough by dipping a spoon into it. Take your finger and run it through the sauce coating the back of the spoon. If you can see a line from your finger, the sauce is ready. This will take about 5 minutes.
5. Stir in the salt, pepper, and nutmeg. Stir in the cheese.

Thing to Note:
If you set your milk out, bringing it to room temperature before you start the sauce, it will cook faster.

Another Thing to Note:
If you don't have white pepper, don't sweat it. Regular black pepper will be just fine. There will just be a couple of specks in your sauce. These add distinction!

Mac and Cheese
Northern Italian Style
serves 4 to 6
20 minutes till it's ready

- 8 ounces dried elbow macaroni, about 2 cups
- 2 cups White Sauce for Mac and Cheese
- 2 ounces Parmesan cheese, shaved, about ½ cup
- coarse black pepper

1. Cook the noodles in a pot of boiling salted water until tender, about 12 minutes.
2. Prepare the White Sauce.
3. Drain the noodles and toss into the pot with the White Sauce.
4. Divide into bowls.
5. Shave Parmesan cheese over the top.
6. Add a fresh grind of pepper to each bowl and dig in!

Americans love their mac and cheese filled with, well, cheese. Lots and lots of cheese. This can be any kind of cheese from the good old bright-yellow processed cheese food (which isn't really cheese) to the trifecta of triple cheeses which feature mostly cheddar, American, and pepper jack. Although any combo of cheese will do, it's all about smoothly incorporating it into the White Sauce. Here's how it's done.

Cheese Sauce for American-style Mac and Cheese

makes about 2 ½ cups
30 minutes till it's ready

- 2 cups White Sauce for Mac and Cheese
- 4 ounces cheddar cheese, grated, about 1 cup
- 4 ounces Monterrey Jack cheese, grated, about 1 cup

1. Prepare the White Sauce. Once it has thickened, turn off the heat.
2. Whisk in the cheddar cheese. When the cheddar has completely melted, whisk in the Monterrey Jack.

Boom! You've got this!

Thing to Note:
Use any cheese you want. You can add more or less based on your personal cheese quotient.

Another Thing to Note:
Notice I used *grated* cheese in the directions for this sauce. Grated cheese will melt faster and easier in the hot sauce than cubes or chunks, although those will still work, you will just need to stir them for a bit longer than directed above.

Now to serve mac and cheese in a bowl, you simply cook your favorite noodle shape then drain and toss the noodles in the cheese sauce. Divide into bowls, and just like that, you've got mac and cheese. Not too shabby!

Most buffet mac and cheese dishes are casseroles where the pasta and cheese sauce are baked together. To accomplish this, we take what we've just learned and add more cheese (along with some other fun ingredients). Let's do it!

VIDEO: Turning white sauce into cheese sauce

You Can Cook Any Thing: Volume 1   51

Baked Mac and Cheese

serves a crowd
1 to 1 ½ hours till it's ready

For noodles:
- 8 ounces dried elbow macaroni, about 2 cups

For sauce:
- ½ cup butter (1 stick), divided (half for the sauce and half for the topping)
- 1 small white or yellow onion, peeled and minced, about ¼ cup
- ¼ cup unbleached all-purpose flour
- 1 teaspoon Dijon-style mustard
- ¼ teaspoon paprika
- 2 cups whole milk
- 1 teaspoon coarse salt
- 1 teaspoon coarse black pepper
- 12 ounces sharp cheddar cheese, grated, about 3 cups (save 1 cup for topping)
- 4 ounces pepper jack cheese, cut into ½-inch cubes, about 1 cup
- 4 ounces mozzarella cheese, cut into ½-inch cubes, about 1 cup
- ½ cup sour cream

For topping:
- 4 slices bread, pulsed into crumbs, about 2 cups
- 2 ounces Parmesan cheese, grated, about ½ cup

1. Preheat your oven to 350°.
2. Coat the bottom and sides of an 11 x 9 x 2-inch baking dish with vegetable oil spray.
3. Cook the pasta in a pot of boiling salted water until al dente, about 8 to 10 minutes. Drain through a colander. Place the cooked macaroni into the baking dish.
4. Melt 4 tablespoons butter in a pot over medium heat. Save the rest for the topping.
5. Add the onion and cook until soft, about 2 to 3 minutes. Stir in the flour, mustard, and paprika until smoothly combined. Pour in the milk and season with salt and pepper.
6. Continue to stir over medium heat until the sauce thickens, about 5 to 8 minutes.
7. Turn off the heat and stir in 2 cups of the cheddar cheese about ½ cup at a time until the cheese has melted into the sauce. Save the rest of the cheese for the topping.
8. Pour the cheese sauce over the pasta and toss to combine. Stir in the cubes of cheese and sour cream. Top all this cheesy goodness with the grated cheddar cheese you saved when making the sauce. (By the way, if you forgot to save the cheese and instead put all of it into the sauce ... don't worry about it. Just keep going!)
9. Melt the remaining 4 tablespoons of butter in a bowl in your microwave oven (or in a pot on your stove top). Stir in the breadcrumbs and Parmesan cheese. Scatter these buttery crumbs over all the cheesy sauce and pasta.
10. Bake until the casserole is bubbling, and the cheese has melted, about 35 to 40 minutes.

"My Way" Ultimate Mac and Cheese

serves a crowd
1 to 1 ½ hours till it's ready

For pasta:
- 8 ounces dried orecchiette pasta, about 2 cups

For sauce:
- 4 tablespoons butter, ½ stick
- 1 small white or yellow onion, peeled and minced, about ¼ cup
- ¼ cup unbleached all-purpose flour
- 1 teaspoon Dijon-style mustard
- 1 teaspoon hot pepper sauce
- 2 cups whole milk
- 8 ounces goat cheese, about 2 cups
- 1 teaspoon coarse salt
- 1 teaspoon coarse black pepper

For add-ins:
- 8 ounces brie cheese, cut into ½-inch cubes, about 2 cups
- 4 ounces Fontina cheese, cut into ½-inch cubes, about 1 cup
- 4 ounces cream cheese, cut into cubes, about ½ cup
- 1 cup cooked cauliflower florets, cut into ½-inch pieces
- 1 cup cooked broccoli florets, cut into ½-inch pieces
- 6 slices bacon, cooked and chopped into small pieces, about 1 ½ cups

For topping:
- ¼ cup butter, ½ stick
- 4 slices bread, pulsed into crumbs, about 2 cups
- 2 ounces Parmesan cheese, grated, about ½ cup
- ¼ cup sun-dried tomatoes packed in oil, minced
- 2 cloves garlic, minced, about 1 tablespoon
- 2 tablespoons olive oil
- 2 tablespoons fresh parsley, chopped

1. Preheat your oven to 350°.
2. Spray the bottom and sides of an 11 x 9 x 2-inch baking dish with vegetable oil spray.
3. Cook the pasta in a pot of boiling salted water until al dente, about 8 to 10 minutes. Drain through a colander. Place into the baking dish.
4. Melt 4 tablespoons butter in a pot over medium heat. Add the onion and cook until soft about 2 to 3 minutes. Stir in the flour, mustard, and hot pepper sauce until smoothly combined. Pour in the milk.
5. Stir over medium heat until the sauce thickens, about 5 to 8 minutes.
6. Turn off the heat and stir in the goat cheese until completely melted. Season with salt and pepper.
7. Pour the cheese sauce over the pasta and toss to combine. Stir in the cubes of brie, Fontina, and cream cheese. Stir in the cauliflower, broccoli, and bacon pieces.
8. Cover the casserole with aluminum foil and bake until the cheese melts, about 30 minutes.

For the topping:
1. Make the topping by melting 4 tablespoons butter in a sauté pan over medium heat. Stir in the breadcrumbs, Parmesan cheese, sun-dried tomatoes, and garlic. Cook, stirring until the breadcrumbs are golden and toasty, about 5 minutes. Remove the pan from the heat.
2. Carefully remove the casserole from the oven. Remove the foil and sprinkle the breadcrumbs over top. Drizzle with olive oil.
3. Place the casserole back in the oven and continue baking until the topping is golden, and the cheese is bubbling, about 10 to 15 minutes more. Be careful not to burn the topping. Your nose will know if the bits begin to burn!
4. Remove the casserole from the oven and sprinkle with fresh parsley. Let it cool a bit before you dig in. Ultimate deliciousness!

Noodle Tubes

Elbow macaroni obviously isn't the only tubular noodle shape. Noodle tubes come in many sizes and lengths, from small penne to large manicotti pasta. Tubes are great because the sauce fills the noodle.

To go along with these different tubes, you can try out some new sauces.

Penne Pasta in Pink Sauce
serves 4 to 6
30 minutes till it's ready

- 2 tablespoons olive oil
- 1 tablespoon butter
- 1 medium onion, peeled and diced, about 1 cup
- 2 cloves garlic, minced, about 1 tablespoon
- 1 cup chicken stock
- 1 (28-ounce) can crushed tomatoes
- 1 cup heavy cream
- ½ teaspoon kosher salt
- ¼ teaspoon crushed red pepper flakes (more if you like)
- 1 pound penne pasta, about 4 cups
- Parmesan cheese, grated

1. Heat the olive oil and butter in a large pot (or sauté pan) over medium heat. Stir in the onion and cook until soft and turning golden-brown, about 4 to 5 minutes. Stir in the garlic and cook 2 minutes more.
2. Pour in the chicken stock. Cook until the liquid is reduced by half, about 5 minutes more.
3. Pour in the crushed tomatoes and heavy cream. Season with salt and crushed red pepper.
4. Reduce the heat to low and simmer the sauce on the stove while you cook the pasta in boiling, salted water until just al dente, about 10 minutes.
5. Drain the pasta through a colander, saving about 1 cup of the pasta water.
6. Pour the noodles into the pot with the sauce. At this point, you can add the pasta water a little at a time until the sauce is just thick enough to coat the pasta.
7. Cook the pasta in the sauce for 2 to 3 minutes, allowing it to absorb the flavors of the sauce.
8. Serve the pasta in bowls. Garnish with grated Parmesan cheese.

Thing to Note:
Pasta water is used to help you with the consistency of your sauce. It contains the starch from the pasta and is already flavored with salt. The starch acts as "glue" to help the sauce adhere to the noodles.

There are all sorts of things you can do with noodle tubes, but the great thing about them is they can make a quick and easy meal. Here's a recipe that uses one pan to cook noodles and sauce all together at the same time!

Ziti Skillet
serves 4 to 6
30 minutes till it's ready

- 1 tablespoon olive oil
- ½ pound Italian sausage
- 4 large cloves garlic, peeled and minced, about 2 tablespoons
- 1 (14.5-ounce) can diced tomatoes
- 1 (6-ounce) can tomato paste
- 1 teaspoon dried oregano
- 1 teaspoon kosher salt
- ½ teaspoon coarse ground pepper
- 3 cups beef stock
- 12 ounces ziti pasta, about 2 ½ cups
- ½ cup half-and-half (or heavy cream)
- 4 ounces mozzarella cheese, shredded, about 1 cup
- 2 tablespoons fresh basil, chopped

1. Preheat your oven to 500°.
2. Heat the olive oil in a skillet over medium-high heat. Add the sausage and cook until browned, about 3 to 5 minutes.
3. Stir in the garlic and cook for 2 minutes.
4. Stir in the diced tomatoes and tomato paste. Season with oregano, salt, and pepper.
5. Add the beef stock to the sauce and stir in the ziti.
6. Reduce the heat to low and simmer the sauce to cook the pasta to al dente, about 10 to 12 minutes.
7. Stir in the half-and-half and cover everything with mozzarella cheese.
8. Place the skillet into the oven and cook until the cheese melts and bubbles, about 5 minutes.
9. Carefully remove the skillet from the stove. (Use a potholder. The handle will be HOT!) Sprinkle with chopped fresh basil. Serve the pasta right out of the skillet.

Pasta in Italy is served differently than here in the United States. Italians tend to have pasta star in the dish, topping it with a puddle of sauce. Here, we tend to take that pasta and submerge it in the sauce. Whichever you prefer, sauce and pasta are a marriage of texture and flavor. You get to decide whether the pasta swims in the sauce or just dips its toe in the pool! Here's an example of a dish which can go either way.

Lamb Ragu
over Penne Rigate
serves 6 to 8
45 minutes till it's ready

- 2 to 4 tablespoons extra olive oil
- 2 large carrots, peeled and diced into ¼-inch cubes, about 1 cup
- 1 medium onion, peeled and diced into ¼-inch cubes, about 1 cup
- 1 medium red bell pepper, diced into ¼-inch cubes, about 1 cup
- 4 ounces thickly sliced bacon, diced into ¼-inch cubes, about 1 cup
- 1 pound boneless lamb shoulder, cut into ½-inch pieces
- 1 cup red wine
- 1 cup beef stock
- 1 (28-ounce) can diced tomatoes
- 1 bay leaf
- 1 teaspoon kosher salt
- 1 teaspoon coarse black pepper
- 1 pound penne rigate, about 4 cups
- Pecorino Romano cheese, grated

1. Heat 2 tablespoons olive oil in a large pot over medium-high heat. Add the carrots, onion, and red pepper. Cook until the veggies begin to soften and turn golden, about 5 to 8 minutes. Use a slotted spoon to transfer the veggies to a platter.
2. Add 1 more tablespoon oil to the pot. Add the bacon and cook until the bacon is just crisp and golden. Use the slotted spoon to transfer the bacon to the same platter.
3. Add the lamb to the pot. (You can add more oil, if needed). Cook until the lamb browns on all sides, about 3 to 5 minutes.
4. Scrape the veggies and bacon back into the pot. Pour in the wine. Reduce the heat to medium and cook until most of the liquid disappears.
5. Pour in the beef stock and tomatoes. Bury the bay leaf in the liquid. Season with salt and pepper. Cover the pot with a lid and simmer until the lamb is tender and cooked through, about 30 minutes.
6. Bring a pot of salted water to a boil. Add the pasta and cook according to the package directions. The pasta should be tender but not mushy. Drain the pasta.
7. Divide the pasta into bowls and top with a ladleful of ragu. Grate cheese over the top.

When you are cooking pasta, you have to consider how it finishes. In the previous recipe, the pasta cooks completely, and then we top it with the sauce. In the following recipe, bucatini cooks to the al dente stage (a bit undercooked), and then it finishes cooking in the sauce. Because it's a noodle tube, it will love a nice saucy bath!

Bucatini all'Amatriciana

serves 4
20 minutes till it's ready

- 2 tablespoons olive oil
- 4 ounces pancetta, cut into 1-inch thin julienne sticks, about ½ cup
- ½ medium onion, peeled and diced, about ½ cups
- 2 cloves garlic, peeled and minced, about 1 tablespoon
- 1 (28-ounce) can crushed tomatoes
- 1 teaspoon kosher salt
- ½ teaspoon crushed red pepper
- ½ teaspoon coarse black pepper
- 12 ounces bucatini spaghetti, about 3 cups
- 2 ounces Pecorino Romano cheese, grated, about ½ cup

1. Heat the olive oil in a skillet over medium heat. Add the pancetta and cook until just golden and crisp, about 3 minutes. Add the onion and garlic. Cook for 1 minute more. Pour in the tomatoes. Season with salt and both peppers.
2. Reduce the heat to low and simmer the sauce for 15 minutes while the flavors blend.
3. Cook the pasta in a pot of boiling, salted water. The pasta should be tender and not mushy since it will continue to cook in the sauce. About 8 to 10 minutes will do it.
4. Drain the pasta, reserving about 1 cup of the pasta water.
5. Add the pasta to the skillet, tossing to coat with sauce. If the pasta is too dry, add some of the pasta water to loosen it. Stir in the cheese.
6. Divide into bowls and serve with more cheese.

Make it "My Way":
Other substitutions for pancetta in this dish are julienne slices of prosciutto, soppressata and salami. You can also substitute canned crushed tomatoes with roasted cherry tomatoes..

VIDEO: Roasting cherry tomatoes

Noodle Stacks and Rolls

It used to be if you wanted sheets of pasta, you had to find an Italian specialty shop and beg the proprietor to order them for you. The only way you could get them was by ordering a case of thirty frozen sheets. That's a lot of lasagna! The good news is they were only fifty cents per sheet, and they would last a really long time in the freezer. However, the world has changed! Today you can find fresh pasta sheets in the refrigerated section of your grocery store. These sheets will work perfectly for lasagnas and roll-ups. Although they are a bit more expensive then those frozen sheets, they are much easier to come by.

Lasagna Bolognese
serves a crowd
About 90 minutes till it's ready

Let's flatten out these noodles and see how they stack up!

    Start with lasagna. Basically, lasagna is noodles stacked on top of each other and layered with sauce and cheese. You can use packaged lasagna noodles you boil first to make them soft, you can use "no boil" noodles that cook in the sauce they are layered in, or you can buy fresh pasta sheets and cut them into the lengths and widths that fit your pan. I've made lasagna using all three options, and it's all delish!

For Bolognese sauce:
- 2 tablespoons olive oil
- 1 large yellow onion, peeled and diced, about 1 ½ cups
- 2 medium carrots, peeled, trimmed, and diced, about 1 cup
- 3 medium celery ribs, diced, about 1 cup
- 4 large garlic cloves, peeled and minced, about 2 tablespoons
- 3 pounds ground beef (chuck, brisket, or ground round)
- 1 teaspoon kosher salt
- 1 teaspoon coarse ground black pepper
- 2 cups tomato paste
- 3 cups red wine
- 1 quart beef stock
- 1 teaspoon dried thyme
- 1 teaspoon dried oregano

For béchamel sauce:
- ¼ cup unsalted butter, ½ stick
- 1 large white onion, peeled and diced, about 1 cup
- ¼ cup unbleached all-purpose flour
- ½ teaspoon dried oregano
- 4 cups whole milk
- 1 teaspoon kosher salt
- 1 teaspoon coarse black pepper
- 4 ounces Parmesan cheese, grated, about 1 cup

For lasagna:
- 2 (8.8-ounce) packages fresh lasagna noodles, about 12 (8 x 4-inch) sheets
- 4 ounces Parmesan cheese, grated, about 1 cup

1. Pour the olive oil into a large pot over medium heat. Add the onion, carrots, celery, and garlic. Cook until soft, about 5 to 8 minutes.
2. Add the beef to the pot. Season with salt and pepper and cook until the beef browns, about 10 to 15 minutes.
3. Stir in the tomato paste and cook for 5 minutes more.
4. Reduce the heat to medium, pour in the red wine, and simmer until the liquid reduces by half, about 8 to 10 minutes more.
5. Pour in enough stock to just cover the beef. Add the thyme and oregano. Reduce the heat to medium-low and simmer the sauce. Continue simmering the sauce, adding more beef stock as it reduces. The idea is to create a rich depth of flavor by reducing and then adding stock. This will take you 30 minutes or more for a rich, thick sauce.
6. Heat the butter in a large pot over medium-high heat. Cook the onion in the butter until soft, about 5 minutes.
7. Sprinkle the flour over the onions. Stir in oregano. Slowly whisk in the milk. (This process will go faster if you warm the milk in a separate saucepan.)
8. Whisk until the mixture thickens, about 10 minutes.
9. Season with salt and pepper. Stir in 1 cup Parmesan cheese. Remove from the heat.
10. Preheat your oven to 350°.
11. Ladle enough Bolognese sauce into a deep lasagna pan (or an 11 x 9 x 2-inch baking dish) to coat the bottom.
12. Cover the sauce with lasagna noodles, trimming the sheets to fit into your pan. Ladle sauce over the top of the pasta. Spoon béchamel sauce over the Bolognese sauce. Sprinkle with Parmesan cheese.
13. Continue layering until you fill the pan. Finish with a pasta sheet, Bolognese sauce, and Parmesan cheese.
14. Cover the casserole with a sheet of aluminum foil. Bake for 30 minutes.
15. Remove the foil and bake until the lasagna is bubbling, and the cheese is melted, about 15 minutes more.
16. Remove the casserole from the oven and rest for 15 minutes before you cut it into squares.

Chicken Lasagna with Broccoli Rabe
with Sautéed Mushrooms
serves a crowd
60 minutes till it's ready

For sauce:
- ¼ cup butter, ½ stick
- 1 medium white onion, peeled and finely diced, about 1 cup
- 3 tablespoons unbleached all-purpose flour
- 1 teaspoon dried herbs de Provence
- 1 quart milk
- 4 ounces goat cheese, crumbled, about 1 cup
- 1 teaspoon kosher salt
- 1 teaspoon coarse black pepper

For add-ins:
- 2 tablespoons olive oil
- 1 bunch green onions, thinly sliced, about 1 cup
- 1 pound assorted mushrooms, sliced, about 3 cups
- 1 tablespoon fresh rosemary, chopped
- 1 large bunch broccoli rabe, chopped, about 4 cups

For lasagna:
- 8 ounces ricotta cheese
- 1 large egg, beaten
- 2 (8.8-ounce) packages fresh lasagna noodles, about 12 (8 x 4-inch) sheets
- 8 ounces fresh mozzarella cheese, grated, about 2 cups
- 3 cups cooked chicken breast, diced
- 4 ounces Parmesan cheese, grated, about 1 cup

1. Heat the butter in a large pot over medium-high heat. Cook the onion in the butter until soft, about 5 minutes.
2. Whisk in the flour and herbs de Provence. Slowly stir in the milk. Whisk until the sauce thickens, about 10 minutes.
3. Stir in the goat cheese. Season with salt and pepper.
4. Heat 2 tablespoons of olive oil in a skillet over medium-high heat. Stir in the green onions and mushrooms and cook until the mushrooms begin to brown. Season with fresh rosemary, salt, and pepper.
5. Cook the broccoli in boiling, salted water until crisp-tender, about 3 to 5 minutes. Use a slotted spoon to remove the broccoli from the water and plunge into ice water to stop the cooking process. Drain well.
6. Stir together the ricotta cheese and egg in a bowl.
7. Preheat your oven to 350°.
8. Place a ladle full of the sauce into the bottom of an 11 x 9 x 2-inch baking dish. Cover the sauce with a layer of lasagna noodles, trimming the noodles to fit the pan. Cover the pasta with a layer of sauce. Place ½ of the broccoli and ½ of the chicken on the sauce. Spoon half of the ricotta cheese mixture and ⅓ of the mozzarella on top of the broccoli and chicken.
9. Add a second layer of lasagna noodles. Top with a ladle full of white sauce. Spread all the mushrooms over the sauce. Sprinkle with ½ of the Parmesan cheese and ⅓ of the mozzarella cheese.
10. Place the last layer of lasagna noodles into the casserole. Top with a ladle of white sauce. Layer the remaining broccoli and cheese on top. Sprinkle with the remaining mozzarella. Pour the remaining sauce over the top of the casserole. Sprinkle with remaining Parmesan cheese.
11. Bake until the top of the casserole is golden-brown, and the cheese is bubbling, about 30 to 40 minutes.
12. Allow the lasagna to rest for at least 15 minutes before serving.

Fiery Chili Lasagna

serves a crowd
about 1 hour to prepare and assemble
and another 45 minutes to bake

For chili:
- 1 to 2 tablespoons olive oil
- 2 pounds ground chuck
- 1 teaspoon kosher salt
- 1 teaspoon coarse black pepper
- 1 medium red onion, peeled and diced into ½-inch pieces, about 1 cup
- 1 red bell pepper, seeded and diced into ½-inch pieces, about 1 cup
- 2 large garlic cloves, peeled and minced, about 1 tablespoon
- 1 chipotle pepper in adobo sauce, seeded and finely diced
- 1 (10-ounce) package frozen corn, thawed
- 1 (28-ounce) can diced tomatoes
- 2 tablespoons tomato paste
- 1 (16-ounce) can black beans, drained and rinsed
- 2 or more tablespoons chili powder
- 1 teaspoon ground cumin

For lasagna:
- 2 (8.8-ounce) packages fresh lasagna noodles, about 12 (8 x 4-inch) sheets
- 12 ounces cheddar cheese, shredded, about 3 cups
- 8 ounces sour cream, about 2 cups
- 4 ounces prepared salsa, about 1 cup

For toppings:
- fresh cilantro, chopped
- ripe avocado, diced into ½-inch pieces
- ripe tomatoes, diced into ½-inch pieces
- green onions, sliced
- pickled jalapeño slices

Thing to Note:
You can buy canned chipotle peppers in adobo sauce in the international section of the grocery store. These babies are hot! Take care in handling them. You can use rubber gloves and remember to wash your hands thoroughly. I scrape away the seeds before I chop the pepper. If you leave the seeds, you will have a very spicy chili!

1. Heat 1 tablespoon of the olive oil in a large pot over medium-high heat. Add the ground chuck and cook until browned, about 5 to 8 minutes. Season with salt and pepper.
2. Add the diced onion, red pepper, garlic, chipotle pepper, corn, diced tomatoes, tomato paste, and black beans. Season with chili powder and cumin. You can add more later if you like.
3. Reduce the heat to medium-low and simmer until the vegetables are soft, about 30 minutes.
4. Preheat your oven to 350°.
5. Place a ladle full of chili into the bottom of a deep lasagna pan (or an 11 x 9 x 2-inch baking dish). Top with a layer of lasagna noodles, trimming the noodles to fit the pan. Cover the pasta with a layer of sauce. Sprinkle ⅓ of the cheese over the chili.
6. Stir the sour cream and salsa together in a bowl. Spoon about half of this chili-cream over the cheese.
7. Repeat with noodles, chili, cheese, and chili-cream, ending with a layer of noodles, chili, and cheese.
8. Bake until the cheese is melted and bubbling, about 30 to 40 minutes.
9. Allow the lasagna to rest for at least 15 minutes before serving.
10. Garnish with cilantro, diced avocado and tomato, green onions, and jalapeño slices.

VIDEO: Handling hot ... hot peppers

You Can Cook Any Thing: Volume 1

You don't have to stack your noodles; you can rock and roll them too! Any of the fillings we use in lasagna recipes can be used to create lasagna rolls. The benefit for these is the helpings are pre-portioned, so they are easy to serve. Also, you can make a bunch of these or enough for just you.

Lasagna Roll-ups

serves 6 to 8
20 minutes prep and about 30 minutes to bake

For sauce:
- 2 tablespoons olive oil
- 1 yellow onion, peeled and diced, about 1 cup
- 1 pound ground Italian sausage
- 1 pound ground round beef
- 2 garlic cloves, minced, about 1 tablespoon
- 1 (28-ounce) can diced tomatoes
- 1 (6-ounce) can tomato paste
- 1 teaspoon dried basil
- 1 teaspoon dried oregano
- 1 teaspoon granulated sugar
- 1 teaspoon kosher salt
- 1 teaspoon coarse ground pepper

For lasagna:
- 1 (10-ounce) package frozen chopped spinach, thawed
- 1 (16-ounce) container ricotta cheese
- 1 large egg
- 2 tablespoons fresh basil, chopped
- 8 ounces Parmesan cheese, grated, about 2 cups, divided
- 1 (8.8-ounce) package fresh lasagna noodles, about 6 (8 x 4-inch) sheets
- 4 ounces mozzarella cheese, grated, about 1 cup

1. Heat the olive oil in a large pot over medium-high heat. Add the onion and cook until soft, about 5 minutes.
2. Add the sausage and beef and cook until browned, about 5 to 8 minutes more.
3. Stir in the garlic, diced tomatoes, and tomato paste. Season with basil, oregano, sugar, salt, and pepper.
4. Reduce the heat to low and simmer the sauce for 15 to 20 minutes, stirring occasionally.
5. Press the spinach through a colander to get rid of as much moisture as possible. Place the spinach into a bowl. Stir in the ricotta cheese, egg, basil, and 1 cup of Parmesan cheese.
6. Preheat your oven to 375°.
7. Place a ladle full of sauce into the bottom of an 11 x 9 x 2-inch baking dish.
8. Place one noodle sheet on your work surface. Cut in half lengthwise to create 2 long noodles. Spoon sauce over one noodle. Top the sauce with some of the ricotta cheese. Sprinkle with mozzarella cheese. Roll the noodle over the filling and place seam side down into the pan.
9. Repeat with the remaining noodles and filling.
10. Drizzle the top of the roll-ups with the remaining sauce and Parmesan cheese.
11. Bake until the cheeses melt and bubbles, about 25 to 30 minutes.

Veggie Noodles

Whether you stack them or roll them, if you stuff them with delicious fillings, your noodles will always be your go-to comfort food. Unless, of course, you decide to venture into veggie "noodles." Let's explore some more.

When the first spiralizer hit the market, I must admit I was smitten. I bought one. Then I bought one which was an attachment to my mixer. Then I bought one for everyone as a holiday gift. Then I bought one as my preferred wedding gift (on the couple's registry or not!). And then ... spiralized veggies hit the grocery store produce shelves, and my spiralizer became obsolete.

It's so easy nowadays to pick up veggies pre-cut into curly noodle shapes, these recipes have actually become easier than making pasta dishes! Because they are vegetables, these "noodles" cook more quickly than dry pasta noodles, yet they act as the same canvas for any sauce you want to make. Here's a couple of recipes to get you started.

Roasted Beet Noodles
with Red Onion and Orange-Maple Glaze
serves 4 as a side
30 minutes till it's ready

- 2 large beets, spiralized, about 3 cups
- 1 large red onion, peeled and sliced into thin rings, about 1 ½ cups
- 2 tablespoons olive oil
- 1 teaspoon kosher salt
- 1 teaspoon coarse black pepper
- 2 tablespoons maple syrup
- 2 tablespoons balsamic vinegar
- zest from ½ orange, about 1 tablespoon
- fresh parsley, chopped

1. Preheat your oven to 425°.
2. Place the beet noodles and red onion rings on a baking sheet. Toss with olive oil, salt, and pepper.
3. Bake until the veggies are soft, about 20 minutes. Remove the beets from the oven and place into a serving dish.
4. Stir together the maple syrup, balsamic vinegar, and orange zest. Drizzle the sauce over the noodles. Garnish with fresh parsley.

Zucchini Noodles
with Pesto and Ricotta Cheese
serves 4
20 minutes till it's ready

For pesto:
- 1 bunch fresh basil leaves, about 2 cups
- ¼ pound fresh spinach leaves, about 1 cup
- ½ cup pine nuts, toasted
- 4 cloves garlic, peeled, about 2 tablespoons
- 4 ounces Parmesan cheese, grated, about 1 cup
- 1 teaspoon coarse salt
- 1 teaspoon coarse pepper
- ½ cup olive oil

For zucchini:
- 2 large zucchinis, spiralized into long curly "noodles," about 4 cups
- 2 tablespoons ricotta cheese

1. Place the basil, spinach, pine nuts, garlic, and Parmesan cheese into a food processor (or blender). Pulse to emulsify.
2. With the machine running, slowly pour in the olive oil to form a paste. Season with salt and pepper.
3. You will have more pesto than you need for this recipe. It will keep in an airtight container in your fridge for several weeks.
4. Cook the zucchini in a pot of boiling, salted water until just crisp-tender, about 2 to 3 minutes. Drain and return to the pot. Turn off the heat.
5. Stir in 2 tablespoons of the pesto. The pesto will melt over the zucchini. You can add more pesto, if you like.
6. Transfer to a serving bowl with a dollop of ricotta cheese over the top.

VIDEO: Making pesto

Honey Roasted Spaghetti Squash
with Spinach and Sun-dried Tomatoes

serves 4
60 minutes till it's ready

For squash:
- 2 medium spaghetti squashes
- 2 tablespoons honey
- 1 tablespoon olive oil
- 1 teaspoon kosher salt
- 1 teaspoon coarse black pepper

For sauce:
- 2 tablespoons roasted garlic butter (see note)
- ¼ cup sun-dried tomatoes, packed in oil, drained, and diced
- ¼ pound fresh spinach leaves, chopped, about 1 cup
- 2 tablespoons toasted pine nuts
- 3 to 4 basil leaves stacked on top of each other and rolled into a cigar-shaped tube, sliced into thin circles
- Parmesan cheese

1. Preheat your oven to 375°.
2. Cut the squashes in half and remove the seeds and pulp. Place onto a baking sheet, cut-side facing up. Drizzle the flesh of the squashes with honey and olive oil, and season with salt and pepper. Flip the squashes and bake cut-side down until soft, about 30 to 40 minutes.
3. Melt roasted garlic butter in a large skillet over medium heat. Stir in the sun-dried tomatoes. Add the spinach leaves and cook until they wilt, just a minute or two.
4. Keep the sauce warm.
5. Use a fork to pull strands from the cooked squash that resemble thin angel hair pasta. Add these to the pan and toss with the sun-dried tomatoes and spinach. Season with more salt and pepper.
6. Transfer to a serving bowl and garnish with pine nuts, thin strips of basil, and shaved Parmesan cheese.

Thing to Note:
The rich flavors of roasted garlic and butter add to the deliciousness of this sauce.

VIDEO: Cutting and roasting spaghetti squash

Roasted Garlic Compound Butter

- 4 large heads garlic
- 2 tablespoons olive oil
- 1 teaspoon ground oregano
- ½ teaspoon kosher salt
- ½ teaspoon black pepper
- 4 tablespoons butter, room temperature

1. Preheat your oven to 375°.
2. Cut off about ¼ of the tops of the bulbs and discard. Place the bulbs on a sheet of aluminum foil, cut side up. Drizzle with olive oil and season with oregano, salt, and pepper. Close the foil loosely around the bulbs, leaving a hole at the top.
3. Place into the oven and bake until the cloves are golden, soft, and climbing out of their papery skins, about 40 to 45 minutes. Remove from the oven and cool to room temperature.
4. Place the butter into a small bowl.
5. Squeeze the cloves from the garlic heads into the bowl with the butter. Discard the papery shell. Use a fork to mash everything together.
6. Spread the garlic butter on a piece of plastic wrap. Use the wrap to roll the garlic butter into a (2-inch) cylinder, twisting the ends to make a tight roll. Place the butter into the fridge to firm.
7. Slice the butter into rounds and place on grilled meats, fish, or veggies.

Thing to Note:
Toast pine nuts by placing them into a skillet over medium heat. You can move the skillet around to roll the nuts on the bottom of the pan. Watch closely, as the nuts will toast (and burn!) quickly. Once they are fragrant (and you will love that aroma), they're done! Remove the nuts from the skillet right away to avoid burning.

VIDEO: Making compound butter

Another Thing to Note:
When you stack basil leaves, roll them into a cylinder and then thinly slice them; it's called chiffonade. Just wanted you to know!

VIDEO: Toasting nuts

VIDEO: Chiffonading

Just to put things all together, let's take fresh veggies and turn them into fresh veggie pasta. All you need is a pasta machine. What do you think ... ?

A Rainbow of Fresh Pasta

serves 4
60 minutes till it's ready

- 2 large eggs, plus 1 egg yolk
- ½ cup spinach puree (substitute with beet, carrot, or your favorite)
- 2 ½ cups unbleached all-purpose flour
- 1 teaspoon kosher salt

1. Use a fork to combine the eggs and yolk with the puree of your choice in a small bowl.
2. Place the flour on your work surface. Use your impeccably clean hands to scoop the flour into a circle. Make a well in the center of the flour. Pour the liquid ingredients into the well.
3. Use a fork to combine the flour into the wet ingredients, starting from the center of the well and working your way to the outside.
4. Use your hands to gently knead the dough into a smooth circle.
5. Cut the dough into four pieces.
6. Flatten each with your hand and run through a pasta machine on the thickest setting.
7. Do this twice and then move to the next setting until you get a thin sheet of pasta.
8. Run this sheet through the machine on the final setting that cuts the pasta into the noodle size of your choice.
9. Dry the pasta for several minutes (or longer) on a rack or swirl the noodles on a baking sheet lined with a bit of flour.
10. Cook the pasta in salted, boiling water for just a few minutes until the pasta is tender.
11. Drain and top with your favorite sauce.

Make It "My Way":
To make the puree, cook (boil or steam) the vegetable until it is incredibly soft. Drain the vegetable thoroughly in a colander and squeeze out as much liquid as you can. Place the veggie into a food processor or blender and pulse to puree. Mix your puree into the egg yolks and then into the flour.

VIDEO: Pureeing veggies

All Things Food

Now that we've covered all things—eggs, cheese, and noodles—look out for Volume 2. It's all about Salads and Veggie Things ... what fun!

Want even more?

Go to Jorj.com and sign up for the I CAN COOK ANY THING app. You'll find instructional videos, links to Jorj's favorite products, more recipe substitutions, ways to use leftovers, menu suggestions, party plans and so much more.

There's a whole community of support just waiting for you to join in!

Come along!!!!

Milton Keynes UK
Ingram Content Group UK Ltd.
UKHW052224150124
436075UK00003B/78